COPING WITH PSYCHOSIS AND SCHIZOPHRENIA

'When feeling bewildered and alone, with a sense of responsibility for a much loved relative affected by psychosis, the testimonies of others with caring experiences can be a lifeline. Professionals and students will also deepen their understanding by learning from carers. The authors have assembled, in this slim volume, a richly varied selection of personal accounts of caring, which will prove an invaluable resource for anyone concerned with compassionate care.'

Philippa Garety, Professor of Clinical Psychology,
King's College London

'This excellent book brings together unique perspectives and insights from a variety of relatives and care-givers who share the experience of having a loved one with psychosis. It will help others to understand the associated struggles and some of the ways people have been able to cope with these challenges. It should inspire hope and action for families and professionals alike.'

Anthony P. Morrison, Professor of Clinical Psychology,
University of Manchester

Coping with Psychosis and Schizophrenia

Family Stories of Hope and Recovery

JULIANA ONWUMERE
King's College London

DAVID SHIERS OBE
University of Manchester

ELIZABETH KUIPERS OBE
King's College London

Shaftesbury Road, Cambridge CB2 8EA, United Kingdom

One Liberty Plaza, 20th Floor, New York, NY 10006, USA

477 Williamstown Road, Port Melbourne, VIC 3207, Australia

314–321, 3rd Floor, Plot 3, Splendor Forum, Jasola District Centre,
New Delhi – 110025, India

103 Penang Road, #05-06/07, Visioncrest Commercial, Singapore 238467

Cambridge University Press is part of Cambridge University Press & Assessment,
a department of the University of Cambridge.

We share the University's mission to contribute to society through the pursuit of
education, learning and research at the highest international levels of excellence.

www.cambridge.org
Information on this title: www.cambridge.org/9781911623694

DOI: 10.1017/9781911623700

First published 2024

A catalogue record for this publication is available from the British Library

A Cataloging-in-Publication data record for this book is available from the Library of Congress

ISBN 978-1-911-62369-4 Paperback

David Shiers is expert advisor to the National Institute for Health and Care Excellence (NICE) centre for guidelines. The views expressed are those of the authors and not necessarily of any employers or organisations linked to the editors, including NICE and the National Institute for Health and Care Research (NIHR).

Can someone navigate please!

This journey is difficult to navigate

There is no roadmap

There is thick fog

The possibility of stumbling, inadvertently into the obstacles, barriers, and roadblocks?

Are there any directions from those with the lived experiences and or the experts with science behind them?

Me, in between, pushed, pulled, malleable and worn out . . . longing for navigation to support such a journey.

Agnes

CONTENTS

ABOUT THE AUTHORS

Dr Juliana Onwumere is a consultant clinical psychologist in the South London and Maudsley NHS Foundation Trust in London, and a Reader in clinical psychology in the Department of Psychology at the Institute of Psychiatry, Psychology and Neuroscience, King's College London, United Kingdom. A key component of her research and clinical work focuses on family-related issues in psychosis, including developing and evaluating support interventions for families and providing specialist family-focused training for healthcare staff. Juliana developed the first massive open online (global) course focused on information and support for those caring for people with psychosis and schizophrenia (www.futurelearn.com/courses/caring-psychosis-schizophrenia). She has authored several academic papers and book chapters on family-related issues in psychosis.

Dr David Shiers OBE was previously a general practitioner (GP) in Leek, North Staffordshire, UK. David has been campaigning for mental health care reform since the late 90s when his daughter was given a diagnosis of schizophrenia in her late teens. Derived from what he felt was lacking in his daughter's early experiences of care, David changed his career, leaving general practice to co-lead the UK's National Early Intervention in Psychosis Programme through the era of the National Service Framework. Now 'sort of retired', Shiers continues to challenge why people like his daughter should accept poor physical health. He has taken part in several relevant National Institute for Health and Care Excellence (NICE) guidelines and quality standards including, most recently, the NICE guideline on rehabilitation for adults with complex psychosis. He has also been a clinical advisor to the UK National Audits of Schizophrenia since 2011. David has been acknowledged by the Royal College of Psychiatrists with the President's medal in 2012, and as 'Carer of the Year' in 2015. He was awarded an OBE in 2016 for services to vulnerable people.

Elizabeth Kuipers OBE is Professor Emerita of Clinical Psychology at the Institute of Psychiatry, Psychology and Neuroscience, King's College London and, until 2012, was an honorary consultant clinical psychologist in the South London and Maudsley NHS Foundation Trust. She was the Chair of the National Institute of Health and Care Excellence (NICE) psychosis and schizophrenia updated treatment guideline for England and Wales in 2014 and 2009. Elizabeth was head of the Psychology department at King's College London from 2006 to 2012 and a founding director of the PICuP clinic (Psychological Interventions Clinic for Outpatients with Psychosis) at the South London and Maudsley NHS Foundation Trust. Her research interests are in developing and understanding interventions in psychosis, family interventions and individual cognitive behavioural therapy (CBT). Elizabeth has authored and co-authored more than 400 articles, book chapters and books, and has more than 40,000 citations for her work. She has led large-scale, randomised controlled trials investigating the efficacy of CBT and family interventions for psychosis. She is a National Institute of Health Research (NIHR) Senior Investigator Emerita. In 2013, she received a Women in Science and Engineering (WISE) lifetime achievement award as well as a lifetime achievement award from the Professional Practice Board of the British Psychological Society. In 2018, as part of the New Year Honours List, Elizabeth was awarded an OBE for services to psychosis research, treatment and care.

PREFACE

The families and informal support networks of people living with a psychotic disorder are not necessarily blood relatives, but are commonly close relatives, namely parents, partners, siblings, or young or adult children. They are typically and collectively referred to as either *informal carers, carers, caregivers, relatives* or *families*. These are generic terms employed to denote the fact that they are providing support and care, but not in a professional or paid capacity. Further, the term 'carer' (and all its variations) is not universally defined, or always readily accepted or used by those in a caregiving role or by care recipients. The common course of a psychotic disorder, with its typical relapsing and remitting pattern, often means the carer role will be a long-term and, for some, a lifelong commitment.

The important role carers can play in facilitating better health and social outcomes for their relatives living with psychosis is widely acknowledged, including amongst people living with psychosis (sometimes referred to as service users), and by health services and staff. The role involves varied behaviours, including creating social environments to provide practical support, encourage recovery efforts and build confidence. Carers can be instrumental in accessing relevant mental health services at first illness onset and during a crisis (Del Vecchio et al 2015), supporting service user engagement with services and treatments, and improving treatment outcomes (Garety et al 2008; Doyle et al 2014). Carers can also significantly reduce levels of relapse and the number and length of psychiatric hospital admissions (Norman et al 2005). The social networks for many people living with psychosis will include a greater proportion of carers (e.g., Palumbo et al 2015). Evidence indicates that life expectancy rates can be significantly higher in people living with psychosis with carers compared to those without a carer (Schofield et al 2001; Revier et al 2015). In addition, the estimated cost savings from carers to national budgets are substantial, exceeding one billion pounds per annum (e.g., The Schizophrenia Commission 2012). Evidence of their importance is further reflected across a broad range of treatment guidelines and recommendations for psychotic disorders (e.g., NICE 2014) and health and social care policies.

While carer experiences are highly subjective, almost all will assume their role with minimal or no time to prepare and without a manual or template on what one should do for the best for their relative, for themselves and for key others in their network (Kuipers 1992). A caregiving role in psychosis and doing things that are seemingly helpful for the service user and/or the carer can be largely based on trial and error, persistence, endurance, resilience, good fortune and the support and understanding from others. Informal caregiving roles are characterised by several experiences and emotional reactions that can present in one sitting or fluctuate, in parallel or independently, with the illness course. We know that many carers report high levels of psychological distress and poorer levels of positive wellbeing when compared to the general population (Gupta et al 2015a; Sin et al 2021). Further, psychological distress levels are particularly raised during the first illness onset, at times of relapse and crises, and during a psychiatric hospital admission, particularly if it was an involuntary admission (Kuipers et al 2010). Based on World Health Survey data from 48 countries, carers are at a higher risk for experiencing psychotic experiences (Koyanagi et al 2022). Approximately one third of carers experience clinical depression (Kuipers & Raune 2000; Prasad et al 2024). Reports of burnout and exhaustion (Onwumere et al 2018a; McKenna et al 2022), trauma (Kingston et al 2016), loss and grief (Patterson et al 2005), and social isolation (Hayes et al 2015) are not uncommon in carers in psychosis. Moreover, some carers might also be dealing with additional challenges in their role that include service user aggression and violence (Onwumere et al 2018b; Smith et al 2018; Onwumere et al 2019; Wildman et al 2023), and/or other types of anti-social, problematic and risky behaviours such as substance misuse (Winklbaur et al 2006). Carers are more likely to miss several days each year from their work and leave their paid roles because of caregiving responsibilities (Gupta et al 2015b; Mittendorfer-Rutz et al 2019).

Data from studies across the globe confirm that the challenging aspects of the caregiving role are evident across all types of carers, including spouses and parents (Jungbauer & Angermeyer 2002); siblings (Bowman et al 2017); children (Cooklin 2018); carers from different ethnic, racial and cultural backgrounds (Jagannathan et al 2011; Alyafei et al 2021); and LGBTQ communities (Martin et al 2019, Worrell et al 2023). Not dissimilar to a person living with psychosis, carers can experience stigma, isolation and exclusion from others that might include acquaintances, but also close friends and relatives, and a generally felt sense of disempowerment (Adelman et al 2014). Mental health problems, particularly severe mental illnesses such as psychosis, are frequently associated with myths and inaccuracies about the groups affected and their underlying causes, which fuel stigma. Stigma and fear of negative judgement from others can make it harder for carers to seek support from others and share their experiences. Opportunities to speak with and be supported by other carers and supportive others can be important for promoting positive wellbeing and feeling valued.

It is important to note that for many carers, their experiences are not uniformly perceived as negative and can include positive, uplifting and transformative experiences, in parallel (Jordan et al 2018; Campos et al 2019). Such experiences are varied and idiosyncratic, but might include a sense of restored hope, pride, and improved self-worth and self-esteem which, in part, reflect their efforts in being able to offer support to their relative. The positive aspects might also include a new appreciation or deeper understanding of the difficulties faced by those living with disabilities or an improved relationship with the relative they support. Unfortunately, however, our understanding of these types of carer experiences and, more broadly, carer perspectives on what they find beneficial in their caregiving journeys has remained largely neglected in mainstream literature and/or limited to discussions in support groups and carer-only platforms. In our professional and personal lives, we have the privilege of meeting many carers from all walks of life. A key commonality is the uniqueness of their life experience and the areas they noted as having helped.

The next few chapters provide a series of first-hand accounts from carers where they candidly summarise some of their experiences and ideas on what has helped in their own coping efforts and personal recovery journeys. The accounts are written by a broad range of carers including those who are parents, siblings and partners, and from varied socio-demographic backgrounds, including race and ethnicity. Some accounts describe experiences and mental health services from several years ago, while others capture more recent events and current service provision. There are accounts that coalesce around a specific event, while other accounts provide a more longer-term narrative. All accounts are offered as personal narratives. Thus, they do not seek to speak for or reflect the experiences of all carers. They are, and must be treated as, individual stories and perspectives on what has happened. Hence, there are and can be no right or wrong narratives, but only authentic accounts that provide an insight into the lived realities of being in a caregiving role in psychosis and factors identified as having been helpful. It is possible that you might be reading these accounts as someone in a caregiving role and are curious to see what other people have said. Likewise, you might be a healthcare professional (or student), service user or simply just someone interested in families and relationships. Irrespective of who you might be, these accounts offer a valuable insight into a much-neglected group. The accounts have been broadly organised around the type of caregiving relationship, for example, parental, sibling, partner caregivers. All authors are identified by the first name of their choice, which for some is their first name or a name that has meaning to them. Across all accounts, issues of confidentiality and anonymity were observed.

ACKNOWLEDGEMENTS

We want to thank all authors for their contributions and all those in informal caregiving roles.

1 UNDERSTANDING PSYCHOSIS AND SCHIZOPHRENIA

Julia Lappin*, Juliana Onwumere and Robin Murray†

Background

Psychosis is the generic name given to a range of illnesses that can affect the mind and interfere with how a person thinks, feels and behaves. The term psychosis covers several different conditions, for example, drug-induced psychosis, psychotic depression, schizoaffective disorder and schizophrenia spectrum disorders. The precise name used can change over time and will depend upon the pattern and length of difficulties that an individual has. A diagnosis of schizophrenia is considered the most severe type of psychotic illness and almost one person in every hundred people will be diagnosed at some point in their life. It used to be thought that schizophrenia was a discrete illness that was quite separate from other psychotic illnesses such as depressive psychosis.

* Julia is an associate professor and psychiatrist at the University of New South Wales, Sydney and Consultant Psychiatrist at South Eastern Sydney Local Health District. As Clinical Director of the New South Wales Tertiary Referral Service for Psychosis, Julia focuses on improving outcomes for people living with psychotic illness.

† Sir Robin Murray is Professor of Psychiatric Research at the Institute of Psychiatry, Psychology and Neuroscience, King's College London and is ranked as one of the most influential researchers, globally, in psychiatry and schizophrenia research. He treats individuals with psychotic illnesses particularly schizophrenia and bipolar illness at the National Psychosis Unit, South London and Maudsley NHS Foundation Trust. He was Chair of the Schizophrenia Commission which, over 2011 and 2012, reviewed in detail the care of people with schizophrenia conditions in England. The Commission made several important recommendations to advance the improvement in the lives and care people with psychosis and their families. He was knighted in 2011 for his services to medicine.

However, we now have a much clearer understanding of how these illnesses can merge into one another without clear boundaries. For example, some people will receive a diagnosis of schizoaffective disorder to reflect the presence of symptoms of schizophrenia and mood disturbance. For such a person, it will not be uncommon or unusual to present with symptoms and experiences which are suggestive of a diagnosis of schizophrenia on one occasion, but schizoaffective disorder or even bipolar disorder on another.

For some people, psychosis will typically have its first onset in late adolescence and young adulthood. This can usually be a time when a young person is navigating significant developmental and social milestones, such as going to college, embarking upon new relationships or employment. The first onset, however, can also occur during middle age and older adult (60+) years. People from all different sections of society, including all social classes and levels of wealth, can develop psychosis. Evidence has shown that reported rates of psychosis can vary substantially across different populations, countries and regions. For some, psychotic illnesses might be a single, one-off, episode, whereas for others it can be a longer-term condition characterised by alternating periods of remission and relapse, and for others again there may be continuous symptoms even when taking treatment. Psychosis is a complex condition that can often be misunderstood and associated with high levels of stigma and social exclusion. It can also be associated with high levels of distress for the person living with the diagnosis, but also for their families and friends.

Key Common Symptoms

A person living with psychosis may experience a range of symptoms, which are typically described as *positive* or *negative*. Positive symptoms refer to experiences that have been *added* to an individual's functioning and will include symptoms described as delusions, hallucinations, disorganised speech or thinking, and confused or disorganised behaviour. Delusions are considered as unusual and bizarre beliefs that are typically based on a misinterpretation of perception or experience. These beliefs can and do vary significantly from one person to another, in terms of their content, associated distress and the impact on different areas of their lives. In persecutory delusions, for example, individuals have beliefs that another (or others) is conspiring against them. In turn, this can lead to feelings of suspicion, fear and emotional distress, and adopting behaviours they believe will keep them safe and protect them from perceived harm. Hallucinations comprise felt experiences in any of our five senses that are not truly there but are experienced exactly as if they are. Hallucinations can be auditory (hearing voices or sounds); visual (seeing things); olfactory (smelling odours); tactile (feeling sensations on the body); and gustatory (experiencing different tastes). Thought disorder and disorganised speech can make it difficult to organise and articulate one's thoughts in a clear enough way for others to make sense of. These types of difficulties can also prevent logical decision-making.

In contrast to the added quality of positive symptoms, negative symptoms describe experiences that are absent from a person's usual functioning. It refers to the loss of ability to function in everyday tasks, such as bathing and self-grooming, cooking, cleaning and being employed or in education. These types of symptoms also include significant difficulties in establishing, maintaining and actively participating in social relationships and activities. Those affected by negative symptoms will tend to lack motivation and the wherewithal to engage in any activities. They will isolate themselves from others and social situations, including family and friends, and will experience a loss of emotions and emotional expression. Negative symptoms, compared to positive symptoms, tend not to receive as much attention from mental health services, professionals and researchers, and can seemingly present as being less distressing to the individual, who may appear to not even notice them. They will, however, be very noticeable to others in their network, including their families. These types of symptoms can be extremely upsetting to observe and may not always be readily understood as being part of the mental health problem. Instead, they can frequently be misunderstood as examples of laziness, rudeness and not caring, which can often lead to conflict with others, including families and the professionals they might work with.

Mood disturbances, such as anxiety and depression, are also common in individuals living with schizophrenia and related psychosis conditions.

For example, approximately more than half of those affected will experience a depressive condition at some point over the course of their illness. Like negative symptoms, mood difficulties can often be overlooked as our attention is focused on positive symptoms. Cognitive skills, such as memory, attention, concentration and processing speed that people require to function and complete day-to-day tasks, will often be disrupted in psychosis. In addition, sleep disturbances (e.g., spending less time asleep, nightmares) can be common, with some individuals being awake and asleep at opposite times to most others. For example, they might be awake through much of the night and have short episodes of sleep during the day.

The experience of an individual symptom (e.g., hearing voices) does not automatically mean that someone has a psychotic illness. This is because individual symptoms are more common than a diagnosis of psychosis and many people experiencing an individual symptom may not experience any related difficulties that bring them into contact with services. When psychosis symptoms first develop, many people can become preoccupied with specific issues and lose interest in key areas of their lives such as friendships, study, employment and previously enjoyed activities. They may behave in ways that increasingly appear odd and out-of-character, and are gradually of concern to those closest to them. Initially, the symptoms may seem to come and go and will often be noticed first by family or friends, while the person themselves would not share their concerns. In the absence of accessing the appropriate supports, treatments and care, most people will become more impacted by their symptoms and experience what is commonly called an acute episode or a breakdown.

Causes

Anyone can develop a psychotic illness and some groups can have an elevated risk of doing so. In schizophrenia spectrum disorders, evidence suggests that men have a greater likelihood of being diagnosed and will tend to be slightly younger at the time of the first onset of the illness. Based largely on data from regions such as Europe and North America, a higher risk of difficulties also exists in racial and ethnic minorities and migrant groups, particularly those from Black communities, a higher risk of difficulties also exists. If someone in a family has a diagnosis of psychosis, there is, statistically, an increased probability of developing it. This risk, however, varies significantly depending on how closely related the family members are. Thus, most people living with a diagnosis will have no family history of psychosis. Living in larger cities has been linked to higher risk, and the longer the individual has lived in the city, the greater the risk.

There is no single identifiable cause of psychosis. It is widely understood to be attributable to a range of different factors that will vary, in relevance and degree, from one person to another. We know that people may become more susceptible to developing psychosis if they have been exposed to a combination of risk factors, which can be psychological, social or biological. Schizophrenia spectrum disorders, for example, are believed to be partly a neurodevelopmental condition. This means there are likely to be factors present in an individual's early life and childhood that affect how the mind and brain develop and render a person more vulnerable to developing schizophrenia-related disorders at a later stage.

In the last few years there has been considerable progress made in increasing our understanding about the causes of psychosis. A range of early environmental factors can also elevate the risk of developing schizophrenia spectrum and related psychosis conditions. Some of these include viral infections, pregnancy and birth complications, stress, trauma and substance (mis)use (e.g., cannabis, cocaine, amphetamines). For example, there is consistent evidence that supports an association between cannabis use and schizophrenia spectrum disorders, with a five times greater likelihood of developing psychosis in people who smoke high-potency cannabis (e.g., commonly described as skunk in some countries) compared to those who do not. The dangers of cannabis are particularly important in adolescents since cannabis use typically predates the development of psychosis rather than being something that people living with the illness use to manage their symptoms.

There has also been some progress in genetic and biochemical research, particularly in identifying genes that might leave an individual more vulnerable to developing psychosis and in understanding how variations in brain chemistry can explain key symptoms. For example, we know that during an acute psychosis episode, an individual releases excessive dopamine (a neurotransmitter) in some brain regions and the degree of dopamine release is related to the severity of positive symptoms that an individual displays. The origins of psychosis do not lie in dopamine anomalies, but such anomalies can help to explain the mechanisms and common pathway underlying positive psychotic symptoms. They may also play a role in the development of negative and cognitive symptoms.

In people living with schizophrenia and related psychosis conditions, nerve cells in parts of the brain may develop faulty connections with other cells. This results in a picture that can almost be likened to a computer with a problem with its wiring. The computer works well most of the time, but when it is overloaded, it can run into difficulties. In a similar vein, when the person living with psychosis is exposed to certain stressors, their brain systems might become overloaded, malfunction, and lead to difficulties such as misreading signals and failing to tell the difference between real and imaginary events. Magnetic resonance imaging (MRI) studies have demonstrated subtle differences in the brain structure between some people with lived experience of schizophrenia spectrum disorders compared to those without.

Health Outcomes and Key Issues

The life expectancy in people living with psychosis conditions is considerably shorter than in the general population. Though exact figures can vary, depending on the study, reduced life expectancy rates can range approximately between 15 and 30 years. The premature mortality in early years is primarily due to higher rates of death by suicide and accidental deaths. However, overall, more premature deaths are caused by physical illnesses, the seeds of which may also be sewn in these early years of illness. High rates of smoking, poor nutrition and inactivity may combine with adverse effects from antipsychotic treatments to increase the risk of dying prematurely from future heart disease, stroke, diabetes and respiratory disease. Tackling these physical health problems requires a 'whole-person' approach from early in the course of psychosis and its treatment – equipping individuals and their families with the knowledge and skills to adopt healthy routines and seek help early if things go wrong. Research efforts focused on improving life expectancy through identifying and minimising risk factors for suicide as well as physical health problems such as diabetes, heart disease and tobacco dependence are ongoing.

Contrary to sensational and stigmatising media headlines (which can fuel discriminatory behaviours and deter people from accessing support), most people with a psychosis diagnosis have not and do not engage in violent and aggressive behaviour. It is often overlooked that they are more vulnerable to being the victims of crime and exploitation by others. However, away from media headlines, we do know that involvement in violent and aggressive behaviours, typically towards people already known to them such as a relative, can be a problem for some people living with psychosis. The factors that can contribute to this risk are varied and, as noted in other areas, differ from one person to another but can include not taking prescribed medication, alcohol and illicit drug (mis)use. It can also relate to specific illness symptoms such as auditory hallucinations, where the voice content might include commands about what the person should do. Developing a detailed understanding of these risk factors can help to support better treatments that can be delivered at an early stage to improve outcomes for those living with psychosis and their families.

Treatments

Psychosis disorders are treatable mental health conditions. The recommended treatments which can be accessed in hospital and community settings aim to support and reduce the negative impacts on those living with psychosis and their families. The aims of treatment have evolved over time: previously, most emphasis was given to reducing positive symptoms. However, contemporary approaches, which are more comprehensive, also aim to focus on the negative, cognitive and mood symptoms, the social impacts of experiencing a mental health problem, and the needs of families.

Across the world, medications (frequently described in services and research as antipsychotics) represent the most common treatment approach used and can play an important role in helping individuals live with psychosis. Thus, at some stage over the course of the illness, those with lived experience of psychosis will be offered and encouraged to take some type of medication to reduce the negative impact of psychosis on their functioning. Medications, their precise names, dosage and how they are administered (e.g., via oral tablets, injection, liquid, nasal spray) will vary from one person to another and across different countries and regions. These variations are influenced by different factors, including the type and pattern of symptoms experienced, individual preference, the degree of understanding, agreement or acceptance of a need for treatment an individual might have, and health systems and medication availability in specific countries. In some countries, for example, an individual living with psychosis and considered by professionals to be significantly impacted by their experiences to such a degree that it affects their functioning might be required to receive medication treatment that they do not, themselves, consent to. Hence, the medications they are offered and might receive will be influenced by the degree to which they consent and agree to take them.

Not dissimilar to medications for any other health condition, medications used in the treatments for psychosis can have some unwanted and/or unintended side-effects. For example, unwanted effects might include experiences such as fatigue, weight gain, excess salivation or disturbances in sexual functioning. Identifying and managing unwanted side-effects are important, as individuals with psychosis (much like anyone else) might be less likely to continue with their prescribed treatments when they have unwanted and unmanaged side-effects. People will often be advised to take medication for an extended length of time that will typically extend beyond a time when an individual feels (or reports feeling) better. The idea is that medications are designed to help people maintain their wellness and reduce the risk of future acute episodes. However, it is not uncommon that people with lived experience of psychosis can find it difficult to continue with their prescribed medications when they feel well or when they have unwanted side-effects, because it no longer makes sense to do so and can feel unnecessary. Stopping medications can also occur when a person does not share the view of others that they have a mental health problem per se or a mental health problem that medication can help with. Unfortunately, not taking medications regularly as prescribed, particularly in the early stages, can often lead to an increased risk of further episodes or exacerbation of their illness experiences and negative impacts for themselves and their families. It can take several attempts to find the right medication (including dose) that best suits an individual and this can often be a difficult process for the individual with psychosis and their families. Over time, the need for medication treatments may lessen and, for some people, the prescribed doses may be decreased or even stopped; however, this should be a slow process with very careful monitoring. These decisions will largely be influenced by how well individuals living with psychosis are getting on in their lives. In other cases, people may benefit from longer-term medication treatment. In these cases, staying on the lowest effective dose of the drug helps to lessen side-effects while also helping with symptoms.

Psychological treatments, which are frequently described as talking therapies, are designed to help people to deal with the symptoms (e.g., delusional beliefs) and/or the common problems associated with symptoms and having a mental health problem such as emotional distress, stigma, and isolation. Different treatments, which can be offered at different points during the illness course, can include individual psychological therapies such as cognitive behavioural therapy for psychosis (CBTp), which is cognitive behavioural therapy, specifically adapted for psychosis. Therapies can also include family therapies and group-based therapies. The groups might include those designed to help with a particular symptom such as coping with voice hearing or an educational and support group, designed to support families and carers and advance their understanding about psychosis. Therapy approaches will vary within their focus, strategies adopted, format, and target group. Moreover, the content of discussions will also vary from one person and one family to another depending on their specific presenting needs and therapy goals. However, despite these variations, psychological therapies are aimed at improving coping efforts and reducing the risk of further acute episodes and crises.

Other types of treatment and interventions that individuals living with psychosis might be offered, are those designed to improve skills needed for everyday living, which are usually negatively impacted by their experiences of psychosis. Such skills might include those involved in attending to self-care, shopping, preparing meals and help in managing their finances and time. Cognitive remediation therapy (CRT) is a form of treatment designed to improve neurocognitive abilities (e.g., organisation and planning skills) among people living with schizophrenia and related psychoses. The goal of cognitive remediation therapy is to improve everyday functioning in people with schizophrenia and related psychoses by improving cognitive processes. Individuals living with psychosis might also receive help and support with developing skills that can assist with securing and/or maintaining voluntary or paid employment roles or undertaking further education and training.

Alongside the important contributions of medications, psychological therapies, life and vocational skills, in the treatments and recovery of people with lived experience of psychosis, are the relationships with close others. Families and informal carers will often remain in close contact with, and/or live together with, the person with psychosis, and their involvement will often continue long after a service or different healthcare professional has ceased contact. They can provide a range of different support functions, including companionship, advocacy and responding to areas of unmet need. Their contributions to improving outcomes and supporting recovery experiences for individuals living with psychosis can be invaluable, but their own experiences and needs can often be hidden and overlooked.

Aisha: A Lived-Experience Account of Psychosis

I dodged the scooter and looked up into the man's face. Hooded and talking, as if to himself, I thought. But it would be his earpiece. His handsome brown face displaying character and vigilance as he weaved amongst the traffic. How magnificent we are, I mused. Black people, all this beauty and culture. Yet here I am, under the 'system', a statistic, another lost soul wandering the halls of a too hot building with bars on their windows. Let out, only to go to the local shopping centre, sometimes accompanied by staff. And what do I buy? Chocolates and fags of course. All that good stuff.

I berate myself for not being healthier, and wonder where this path will lead. Stretching exercises in the garden as people shout, moan and wail. Contorting their bodies to express emotional pain.

My case notes read *aggressive, disillusioned* and *paranoid*. I now remember to sit with my legs folded and hands on my lap, and back up straight. But I am a person, I am a civilised being, and I am not your statistic.

The reasons for my decline are both simple and complicated. An aggressor that I speak nothing of to the mental health team. I don't trust them. They are clinical and seem to only smile at you during lunchtime. Stressed perhaps, or stressed definitely. What difference does it make that they have seen others like me, and they will see more? I glance at my palms looking for a fingerprint, and I laugh, since looking is supposedly a first sign of madness.

What makes me unique? My love of poetry, nature and family. My family, who seem to sit in their middle-class world mocking me, afraid and worried? Mocking is the part of the mind that isn't functioning; all this love I could no longer accept, and it became twisted, dark and fantasised. All I had built had crumbled: my properties, my close group of girlfriends and my love. Shattered, and in ruins. Perhaps this exclusive, elusive world I had occupied was just that, a fragile net waiting for someone to pull at its joining; and there was me, I fell out into a world of poverty, drug-fuelled companions and restless nights. Homeless and nameless. All the heart I had always given to those who suffered, who would give their heart to me now, it is me who is suffering?

I dreamt wildly and manically of all the things that I would do once I was healed. Yet, I pondered, was there one kick too many to the stomach, and could it be reversed? Could I be loving to all again? This question played with me, but jaded and bitter was not an option. So slowly but steadily, I put one foot on the bottom of the ladder and began to climb. Here, today, I go up and down this ladder, but I am again loving, giving and whole. My brain plays tricks, my therapist calls it the 'Tricky Mind', and I have to catch myself when that happens. Yet, in stillness, and the silence of my flat with its pretty plants and the park outside with children filled with joy, it brings me peace and stability. And I realise, it doesn't really matter what I do or what I have in terms of a career, money or fitness. What matters is that I am good. I cringe at the ones who brought this into question and fear their bullying at times. Sometimes, what you stand up against and object to throughout your life, like bullying, can become the very thing that brings you down. However, I stand tall as an oak tree in knowing recovery happens, that health is real and beauty lies in the open hands of waiting and patient family.

2 PARENTAL CAREGIVER ACCOUNTS

Annette

I'm a member of 'the human race', as well as being a mother of four children. My middle child was diagnosed with a mental illness in 2016. I experienced some different emotions during that difficult time. I was so frightened regarding my son's unusual behaviour. I could not understand what was happening, or why this was happening within my family. At times, I felt angry because everything seemed to be out of my control. I began to isolate myself. I could not even tell my family or friends in the first instances; it was too embarrassing. I did not want to speak to anyone. I felt so disappointed in myself; I thought I had failed in my duties as a mother. Sometimes, the feeling of guilt would consume me so much. My stomach would constantly be in pain. My head and heart would always be pounding so loud. My sleeping patterns were altered so much that I could not remember if I managed to close my eyes at times during those bleak nights.

Another significant traumatic experience was when my son was first detained under the Mental Health Act. When he was admitted to a psychiatric hospital, I was so shocked and saddened because I could not help my child. I recalled the first ward round meeting; I was asking myself, why are all these people here discussing my son? There was too much jargon being exchanged in the room from the healthcare professionals. The word 'psychosis' was repeated quite regularly; I felt so scared and lost. It just did not make any sense to me; however, I managed to visit my son every day. I would also call the hospital and speak to a member of staff. I wanted to make further enquiries regarding my child. Sometimes, my son would phone me. The conversations would be very abrupt, while our emotional connection between us seemed to be very strained. The constant visiting was having a terrible effect on me, especially physically. I believed at that time, I was doing the right thing for myself. I still did not understand the procedure regarding being detained in a hospital. On a few occasions, he would phone me back requesting food and a mobile phone. He actually asked me to get him out of 'that hospital'; that request really made me feel so helpless.

Again, I would ask myself, how did I cope? I still do not know if I was coping well but I felt like I was existing on autopilot. It felt like I was living in a 'distorted nightmare' that would not end. Looking back now, I'm very doubtful that I coped well back then. I think I went into survival mode. I just kept pushing forward without any significant direction or ideas. When my son's detention was extended from a Section 2 to a Section 3, I thought this must be very serious now. During that process, a community mental health team was allocated to my son. That team was to be involved with my son's care upon his discharge from hospital. Myself, my other children and friends were offered support from an early intervention psychosis team.

I truly believe that my coping mechanisms began to unfold during a monthly carers' group. That group consisted of a couple of healthcare professionals and some other people who were referred to as carers. Those meetings were invaluable. They provided a confidential non-judgemental space to obtain information about mental health issues. The carers shared their personal experiences coping with loved one(s) who were struggling with mental health problems. I attended the meetings frequently, and heard some harrowing accounts. In my first few meetings, I was so overwhelmed with sadness. I'm sure I just sat there amongst everyone and just cried. However, during one of the monthly sessions, I finally accepted what had happened to my son was not my fault. By accepting the situation, I was slowly beginning to rebuild my own life. Attending the carers' group made me realise that there was support available for myself and my family. I also finally understood what the term 'carer' meant to me. I have done my best for myself, my son and my family. There was a sense of camaraderie amongst the carers; we could relate and empathise with our current circumstances.

Nowadays, I am more confident with myself. I have learnt several strategies to cope as a carer. As much as that journey was very uncertain,

I discovered that doing activities for myself would be so beneficial for my own wellbeing. 'There is light at the end of the tunnel.' I can put my own needs first. It was the only logical way to consider myself first, then I can support others. Sharing and speaking to family, friends, colleagues or healthcare professionals was important. Getting the relevant support really encouraged a better outcome for me. Letting go of the stigma was not easy but it created a better relationship for myself and my son.

I had no choice but to re-establish my own life again. I would socialise more with family and friends. I obtained a brand-new purpose, such as undertaking new courses, training and improving my interpersonal skills. I am currently involved with an acoustic drum kit course, drama, singing, yoga, art, swimming, as well as doing presentations, public speaking, training and co-facilitating two carers' groups.

For me, being active in a variety of situations has assisted me coping with my role as a carer. However, I am very aware of my own limitations. I am mindful of myself in what I can and can't do. By creating a special concept named 'LAM' in 2018, 'Looking After Me', this is my own personal coping plan. Even though, life can be very unpredictable, I always believe 'that a storm will not last forever; I will definitely create my own sunshine that will shine brightly just for me'. I trusted myself greatly, that I can take time out when necessary. I can honestly say that the past was very upsetting, but the future is still very exciting with all the new challenges that will be ahead of me.

Vivien

Over the last 30 years that my husband and I have been caring for our daughter, the most challenging times have been the violent and abusive behaviours, including having abusive phone calls day and night, and being frightened of my daughter's behaviour, physically and verbally. Having to get my daughter sectioned for her own safety and that of others, and not being able to help her, knowing she was in torment, was also challenging.

Visiting her in many different hospitals, and seeing how the care varied enormously, was hard, and more so when the visit included a hostile reception from my daughter. Having to empty her accommodation when she had been hospitalised, and trying to get through to someone who would not talk at all, was hard. Staying strong as parents with so many challenges to deal with was tough, while also trying to lead a normal life. It felt like a totally draining time, which also included convincing the authorities that my daughter was in an abusive relationship with a partner.

Family relationships can be difficult sometimes, but so much more so with mental illness. Over the years, there have been a few things that have helped me. Having a doctor ring up and ask how you are and give you updates on my daughter's progress was important. It made me feel less isolated. During one hospital admission, there was an amazing psychologist. He delved into my daughter's past in great detail. He was trying to work her out; he spoke to her sister who lived in another country. Her sibling had felt that she had lost her sister whom she was close to when they were young.

Going to church, where there is a wonderful group of supporting people who know me well, helped me. It allowed me to try and offload all my worries. I have tried to keep fit by going to a health club. The challenge of the gym classes, and chats over coffee afterwards, have been helpful. Even when the gym was shut during the Covid-19 lockdown, we met up outside, when allowed, and went for walks. Being a keen gardener, I can just go into another world and get completely involved in whatever I am doing. This also gives me a sense of achievement and relaxation. Helping others in the village where we live, and where we have a community café, has been beneficial. It is a place where people can meet and chat.

The love and support of family, including my daughter, has always helped. When my daughter says 'Mum, I do love you. You have always been there for me', it makes all the heartache of so many years melt away, and all my efforts worthwhile.

Raj

Our story relates (belongs) to our daughter's battle with psychosis, her struggles, her fightback and her determination to return to the other side. This is also a story of our struggles as parents and our journey with our daughter's illness. Affectionately, we call her Sani, which means 'little one' in Nepali. Often, for my wife and I, it has also felt like our own illness. However hard it hit us, there is a sense of guilt when talking about our struggles as parents. It pales into comparison to what our daughter went through with suffering the actual illness.

I had initially trained as a paediatrician, then as a general practitioner. Twenty-eight years of experience as a doctor in the UK completely failed me after I spoke on the phone with our daughter, who was holidaying in Nepal at the time. She was confused and what she was saying did not make any sense to me. I replied, we are coming to see you, and tried reassuring her that everything would be okay. We booked the next available flight to Nepal. I knew immediately it was psychosis; but why? It was so unexpected, so unreal and nothing could have prepared us for this situation. My wife and I hugged, and we cried. Although I had come across psychosis many times before, as a GP, I did not know how to deal with it when it affected my own daughter.

When we arrived in Kathmandu, Sani appeared indifferent to us, and it did not register in her mind that we had travelled from the UK. The daughter we had left behind a few weeks earlier was not there. Instead of our loving, kind daughter we found someone very different with whom it was not easy to hold a meaningful conversation. Delusions had become her truth. We had to keep reminding ourselves that this is not Sani but her illness that is talking. It was very painful but our anxiety, strangely enough, lessened to some extent after seeing her in person and knowing that if she was with us, we could protect her, and we were going to look after her, whatever it took.

Sani refused to come with me to see a psychiatrist, so I went alone. It was not difficult for the psychiatrist to make a diagnosis of an acute psychotic episode based upon my description of the events. Our family in Nepal just could not make sense of what was happening, having never seen this before, and were at a loss to understand how to help other, than praying in temples and monasteries. An image still sticks clearly in my mind of my brother placing Sani's medication, when I first brought it home from the chemist, in front of the picture of his Buddhist guru, and praying.

Sani calmed down, started to sleep better and then the three of us returned home to the UK. She stayed at home with us. We would go for walks with her but would hardly talk. It was heart wrenching to see her face in so much pain; even in her smile, pain seemed to pour out. We were just hoping and waiting for better days to return to our lives. There were so many questions and no easy answers. What could have prevented this? We would rewind her life events again and again. Will she ever return to her normal self? Will we ever see again the kind and loving daughter who she was before? Will she ever be able to complete her studies and live independently? Who will look after Sani when we are gone? All kinds of pessimistic thoughts filled our minds. But we knew that we had to persevere and hope for the best. What was never in doubt was our determination to support her and normalise our lives as far as possible. Stress has the potential to break family relationships, but it can also, like it did for us, bring us closer together. This has been a journey where pain, anxiety and paranoia has actually bound us together.

There is so much stigma attached to mental ill health, which can potentially result in discrimination. Although we knew that in order to fight this stigma, we must not hide it. It was easier said than done. We also did not know whether it was right to discuss it with our friends and relatives, when in fact it's our daughter's illness, not ours. However, we mostly kept it to ourselves without intending to hide it. There were times when we felt like shouting it out loud from the rooftops.

What worried my wife and I the most was the thought of Sani relapsing or needing an admission to a psychiatric ward. Sani returned to academic studies to start her masters in a different city. Although we had encouraged her to return, we lived in constant anxiety and paranoia about her wellbeing. This was our illness not hers, and we found it difficult to deal with. In between another couple of minor psychotic episodes, Sani earned her masters' degree. We could not have been prouder parents.

Professionally, my experience with Sani has given me a much better insight into mental health issues. At work, I became even more sympathetic to people who had a history of psychosis. At times, I had difficulty maintaining my composure when dealing with young adults of my daughter's age who were struggling with their mental health issues.

Our journey has been a rollercoaster of a ride, but without regrets, rather there is a sense of inner satisfaction. We appreciate where we have all arrived. Our journey was powered by unconditional love, compassion, desire and hope.

Pat

In 1983, my husband, my children's father who had mental health problems that he refused to acknowledge, left our home. My son was 20 years old, living at home and working. His two younger sisters, aged 15 and 17 years old, were still at school. I also had a new job as a nurse on a medical ward in a local hospital.

I had never known anyone with a psychosis. So, when my son began to say strange things and was obviously distressed but unable able to say why, I was totally at a loss to understand. He began to receive messages from the TV and a house four doors away. He became angry, threatening, uncooperative, uncontrollable and, worst of all, unpredictable.

My son went to see his GP and although he was still living at home with me and his siblings, I was not told what the problem was or what any plan of treatment might be because of confidentiality. He was referred to the local outpatient service of the mental health hospital. I wrote to them asking for help, but the letter I received referred to my son as my husband. My heart sank into my boots, thinking they don't even know what relation he is to me. We had a student social worker visiting our home who, after 10 weeks, said she had come to the end of her course and would no longer be visiting. As a family, we were just left. I was told unless my son hurts anyone or himself, then nothing more could be done.

With the breakdown of my marriage, my children, and an ill elderly mother to care for, and a new job, I felt as though I had half of my local town leaning on me. Over time, my son's mental health and behaviour deteriorated; he lost his job and was putting all the family at risk. He was bringing people in from the street and putting his siblings and myself at risk and accusing us of doing different things, such as working for the government. My youngest daughter was having panic attacks and ready to jump out of the window because she was so frightened. It was these types of events that led to my decision that he would have to go, and I informed his social worker. I was always afraid he would end up on the streets or in prison.

My son has spent different periods living in rehabilitation facilities, family lodgings, living with his elderly grandmother, and in hospitals following being sectioned. He once spent a long time in an old local 'asylum', as it was then described, and this was the worst time in my life. No one had mentioned recovery or what the ward was.

Over the years, my son's father and other relatives abandoned him. My second husband (his stepfather) made a great contribution in rehabilitating him. However, since the death of his stepfather a decade ago, it is just mental health staff and myself who have supported my son. During his illness, I have had 15 really good years with him that have included taking him on holiday, for days out, to meet with friends at a garden centre coffee shop because my son has no friends of his own.

My son, with a 37-year history of mental illness, is now in his late 50s. We have been going through a time when he has told me that he no longer wants to be friends. I am told that he has psychotic thoughts about me but because of confidentiality I am not allowed to know what exactly they are. This has left me feeling bereaved and very sad. There is no family intervention to restore this broken relationship.

In the beginning, having a very supportive general practitioner, kind, helpful police and an understanding solicitor were all helpful for me. Having staff willing to talk to me was important and being able to explain the illness in a way that I understood and being happy to give me information, and not hiding behind confidentiality, also helped. It was staff who listened to me as though I mattered, made me feel valued, saw me as part of the team, and answered my letters.

In the early years, I joined as many carer support groups as I could find and I tried to learn about services, where they were and what they did. Listening to other carers, making friends, and gaining information about their experiences of different doctors and hospital wards was helpful. I read about schizophrenia and eventually about all sorts of mental illness. I worked at making good relationships with staff and supporting them. I became assertively polite in my efforts to get appointments with psychiatrists. I attended meetings involving mental health services. I got involved in research and I gave talks about carers' experiences as part of staff induction training. After my retirement, I then facilitated a carers' support group for 14 years.

Amanda

As a parent you expect to watch your children grow and become independent adults. When this process is not so smooth, you begin to blame yourself. This is a story of how things can change so very easily. It is important to hear the voices of all who are affected within a family circle. I have three sons; my middle son was nearly 20 when I noticed he was getting very agitated over very little things; he seemed irritated all the time and was not sleeping more than two–three hours a night. I tried to get our GP to visit him at home, but when I told my son the doctor was coming, he said there is "*nothing wrong with me*" and "*you see him if you need to, but I am ok*".

Things really came to a head when it was time for his younger brother to transfer from primary to secondary school, which was at a time when I had just been discharged from hospital with a diagnosis of Brugada Syndrome and fitted with a mini defibrillator.

My son had offered to attend the meeting at the secondary school, with his younger brother, to get all the information about transfer. He returned home, letting me know that it had all gone okay, with no problems. The next day, the Deputy Head called me to let me know that my son had stood on the school stage and proceeded to take questions from the floor and explain the admission and school processes to the other families that were visiting. It was his belief that he was in charge.

I knew I had to do something, yet I think I still I buried my head with the hope of "*oh, it will get better*" and "*oh, it will go away*". Nearly two weeks later, there was a family gathering. I was not well enough to attend, but my son did. The day after, I received several phone calls from friends and family asking, "*what is going on*"? During the gathering, my son had been shouting, swearing and accusing others of laughing at him and talking about him. I could no longer ignore what was happening.

With the help of a friend, and my eldest son, I persuaded him to see the GP. When we went, he told the GP, "*I can do your job, you talk to people. I am good at that, there's nothing wrong with me*". Our GP was great and had asked a few questions. My son agreed to go to hospital so the staff can let him know that he was ok. When we got there, he kept pacing up and down and running outside. The hospital staff called the security guards. It was so distressing to see; all the family were in tears, and it was very tough to deal with.

I remember thinking that after a few weeks in hospital and a few pills that it would be better. The doctors kept saying this is a *first* episode, which really upset me because I kept thinking, it is like they are waiting for it to happen again. Eventually, he was discharged, in a series of stages starting off with short periods of home leave, then fully home. We have really had a bumpy ride, but it is more plain sailing now. My son is in a much better space, he is more interactive and has started going out a bit more. As a family, we do talk about our experiences and share them with the wider community, in a way that says it is ok to not be ok.

At the start of this journey, I couldn't think about myself and my needs, all I could think about was making this better. The first thing that I remember clearly, was a friend coming to see me; she brought a fizzy drink and an invite to spend 15 minutes in my local park talking or not, whatever I was comfortable with. We walked and talked, it felt so good to be outside and to talk about normal everyday things. At that point I had hardly left my home. But just to be free, even for such a short time, helped me to see that I had to add myself into this equation or I would not go the distance. Another day, I had a phone call from a friend saying, dancing tonight, be ready for 7.30. I love line dancing but had stopped going because I felt I had to be on duty, or on call. I needed the confidence and support to return to the things I love. I coped by taking small steps, going for half the class, then eventually the whole session. I had taken extended leave from my job; my boss was sympathetic at first, but then one day he asked to have a meeting. He said, very gently, you need to really think about the future; when things improve at home, what are *you* going to be left with? He made some adjustments to my work and allowed me to keep my phone on silent mode, in case of an emergency. This helped me to relax and focus to be the best that I could be, whilst knowing that I could be contacted if needed. My work on a lived experience register, in an NHS health trust, has also increased my confidence.

Today, I am hopeful for the future.

Chris and Terry

It was six o'clock on a warm summer's evening, when my teenage son uttered a sentence that was to change my life forever. I was watching the BBC News, when suddenly my son, Steve, looked up and said, "*The BBC have been talking about me all day*" – my heart missed a beat – I felt sick – I had become a carer.

It was four weeks later when I was awoken in the middle of the night with a sudden almighty crash and the sound of breaking glass – my son was screaming to his voices – "*Fuck off! Fuck off! Fuck off!*" My wife lay next to me crying. "*We have to do something*", she sobbed. "*He needs to go to hospital now, I want my son back, I want my son back*".

That was nearly twenty years ago, and although in all honesty we have not got our son back; he still hears voices and is plagued with anxiety and indecision. Our son is unable to work or make many relationships, but he has learnt to live with his disability and to smile again. However, he would have struggled if it had not been for the support he has had from our family, the kindness of friends and understanding from neighbours.

I asked my wife what she thinks is the most important tip to other carers; her reply was very simple, 'PATIENCE', and lots of it. Things will not happen overnight, it is a long haul, but we think that if you are patient and follow some very basic steps, you can and will get there. The following are some of our key lessons we followed as parents:

1. Learn not to blame yourself – you did not cause the illness, you did not knowingly pass on the genes, you could not watch over your child's every moment – it is not your fault!
2. Read up on your child's diagnosis and treatment – when you understand more about the illness and the treatment, it will help you manage the situation so much better.
3. Talk to other families or join a 'carers' group' (essential in my view!). Talking to other carers was the single most important thing my wife and I did – talk to the local Community Mental Health Team to see if there is a local mental health carers' group.
4. Link up with a specialist charity. If you are stuck in a foreign land and cannot speak the language, having someone with you who can, helps enormously – joining a specialist charity is exactly the same.

5. Arrange for a Carer's Assessment – ask the local mental health team for a Carer's Assessment, it will help you link into the 'system'.
6. Find out about any benefits that you might be entitled to – a minefield but essential. Talk to a specialist charity for advice – you may be entitled to some financial benefits.
7. Find out more about how the mental health system works – essential to know who is who, and what they do.
8. Learn to be proactive and not wait for the services to react. Don't assume the systems will automatically respond; they are mostly rushed off their feet. You very often have to make the first move and be tenacious.
9. Learning to live with psychosis – psychosis is a disability like any other disability; you have to learn to accept and live with it. I wish my son was not disabled, but he is.

Sheena

I sobbed for days, uncontrollably, like an animal howling for the loss of a newborn. My gentle son had attacked us in the middle of the night while staying for the weekend, and nothing made sense any longer. I wandered aimlessly round my friend's garden. I couldn't return home – home was a designated crime scene. In the time it takes to wash the pots, my life had been changed for the foreseeable future. My son would be labelled a mentally disordered offender, and I was seen as a victim. As a mum I didn't see it like that.

I'd phoned the Assertive Outreach Team in the afternoon when I'd gone to pick my son up from his accommodation, as he was staying for the weekend. It was clear he was unwell. Carers know when their relatives are unwell; I was simply assured that he was fine and I should make sure he took his medication. It happened that night. My friend was later to say, 'I don't know how you did it. I used to watch you in my garden, and I couldn't see how you would ever recover from that.' The thing is, when your son ends up in prison when he should be in a psychiatric unit, there's plenty to do. When the tears end, there must be action. The battle to get him moved to a hospital took four months. I use the word battle – carers understand that.

The first time I saw my son, after what was an extremely violent event, was in the prison a fortnight later. I was apprehensive; would such violence have changed how I felt towards him? Would he be changed? Simply put, the answer was no. He was apologetic and struggling to make sense of what had happened. A tearful hug brought us together and set us on the road to recovery.

It was the belief in him as a person that kept me going – not blind love, though love plays a part, but knowing him as a kind, thoughtful and considerate person. The newspaper headline was clear that he had been let down by mental health services, but no amount of complaining could change the situation, however unjust it felt to me. Better use of my time was needed.

Getting to know the secure mental health system became important. That gave me the opportunity to challenge decisions and care provision, where necessary. I had to understand what my son needed to do to move through the system. I had to know my rights as a carer so that my voice was heard. Secure services are not carer friendly, so it was also important to make contact with other carers to lessen feelings of 'being the only one'.

Friends equally played a part in my recovery. I was encouraged by the psychologist I worked with to identify the friend I could talk to, the one who I could do things with, the one who offered practical advice and the one who would make me laugh. It felt a little mercenary at first, but I also lost friends and family who simply didn't know what to say. And crying? I don't do that anymore – the worst has happened; I can survive anything now. There is only the future to look to.

Philippa

Imagine a situation when it feels a relief to hear that your son has schizophrenia, and when it is satisfying to learn that you are a mental health carer. Both these revelations came to me 15 years ago and they felt good because, for the previous eight years, I had been unable to get a diagnosis out of the clinicians who had dealt with my very ill, deluded son, and no one had mentioned that I had a key and recognised role in supporting him. Years had gone by when there was no feeling of partnership with the professionals, and real concerns, such as about the damaging weight gain, which tends to be a side effect of antipsychotic medication, were just brushed aside.

Once we knew the name of his illness rather than just the list of symptoms, it was possible to access information and to get support from people in a similar position. I did this primarily through the charity Rethink Mental Illness, which has as its mission to secure a better quality of life for all those severely affected by mental illness. Attending carers' support groups, helping with projects and campaigns, and eventually becoming a member of its Board of Trustees, were all satisfying and seemed to make some sense of what was, otherwise, just a family tragedy.

Since then, life has had its ups and downs. The downs have included encountering a particularly rude and stigmatising psychiatrist, trying to deal with a whole series of medication errors from a hospital pharmacy, several tussles with the Department for Work and Pensions with their long forms and short empathy, and a severe relapse into psychosis when matters seemed to be going reasonably well. The ups, as time has gone on, have included many helpful professionals, the eventual introduction of a medication which has now worked well for several years and the provision of community activities and therapies.

One of our best decisions was that our son should use some of the benefits money to employ a personal assistant for a few hours a week. We found a resourceful person who helps him to maintain a degree of independence by giving support and practical care, with a lot of emphasis on his physical health. Bracing walks, biscuit-free shopping and regular weigh-ins are all part of the routine.

Above all, I think the key ingredient of successful coping is to do one's best to maintain supportive contact with friends and colleagues who will, above all, listen and maybe advise. Beyond one's own networks, these can be found in formal support groups where, perhaps best of all, one's own experience can possibly help others. A carer's life is not the one that we would choose but it can at least sometimes be interesting.

Agnes

I am a parent of a young adult and, like most parents, I want the best for him and to see him grow and develop, focusing on what makes him smile and brings as much meaning to his life as possible. For over a decade, my son has been battling with psychosis.

A government minister once stated that UK mental health services were not fit for purpose. This helps me to recognise the severe limitations around recovery and that it is not our fault. We do not have the resources and/or the support for holistic recovery. One friend said to me, "*the cavalry is not coming, there is no rescue or recovery plan, you are on your own*". He was not being unkind, just honest in his observations of our situation. Therefore, capturing meaningful moments from our daily lives is necessary to stay hopeful in the here and now, rather than wait for a future which may never come. It is the small acts of kindness which keep my resilience and stamina for the daily battles with the illness, its impact on our lives, and the services which, in reality, often work against us/me. Sitting as companions – my son on his play station, me on my laptop and the sun shining through the window – are significant moments to me. Likewise, making each other a drink, watching light TV (e.g., cookery) programmes are important events. Keeping the day as light as possible, means blocking a lot out. I limit who I allow into our home, and I try to keep each day simple, avoiding, if possible, anything complicated. We often have a little dance together to celebrate blessings like the sunshine or the rain. These small moments help to heal the challenging times, when his beliefs, thinking and behaviours are unusual, and/or difficult to square with reality.

It is challenging for me to work full time as my son wants someone around, particularly if the dominant voice command is being mean and/or he cannot sleep. He gets confused and/or can't remember and can be suspicious of others. Periodically, he has become aggressive towards me; these are usually at times when no services are easily accessible. I have given up ringing the out-of-hours services, as there is a lack of staff, long call waiting times and then they say "*it's a domestic*", and to "*ring the police*". I now have my own measures. I have created a safe room in my bedroom, with a lock and bolt, and I feel very safe there until things calm, which they invariably do. I sleep more soundly knowing this is in place. I also self-fund a lifeline service that allows a friend to be called at the push of a button. My son can overspend and need support managing his money. This feeds into my own insecurities about finances. My son has at times unusual beliefs about home-cooked food and also does not think he is able to cook, so he lives on daily takeaways, which are expensive and unhealthy. He usually looks forward to the food delivery, a highlight to his day. I struggle, as I like to have reasonably healthy meals and recycle. Invariably, he over orders and a lot of food is wasted alongside the plastics and cardboard. I have learnt to surrender to what is and accept this reality.

Following a self-harm incident, he experienced different life-threatening conditions but survived, thanks to modern medicine. This led to challenging behaviours including having electric fires in his room, most of the time to keep warm. This keeps our heating bills high and adds to money worries. Alongside this, is the legalising of CBD which he smokes close to our neighbours' gardens. Am I a snob, and an overprotective parent? If I am, I have had to learn not to be; I hate the smell of this substance, but he resists any challenges about this. I hope my neighbours are tolerant without understanding the complexities of his condition, which I only share if required to.

Due to previous incidents, my son's medication is delivered weekly. If there are changes and/or problems with this, it can lead to misunderstandings. If it is not accurate, he will say he can't take it. I have learnt to psychologically step back and listen. To withdraw, to some extent, and allow his autonomy even when I know possible consequences from past experiences. To trust his judgement and not be overbearing, whilst being alert to my own wellbeing and safety, is key. I am, in fact, anti-medication; I believe it does more harm than good. However, when he lowers them, he becomes unwell, and this results in hospital admissions. We are caught in a vicious circle.

I recently went to a meeting about my son with his mental health team and on the door was a reminder to staff about their mental health, what to look out for and what steps to take. I was pleased to see staff were being looked after, but asked what about the unpaid carer, who works full time and gets no supervision, training and/or time off? What about us? This is the invisible world we navigate to protect the public purse, our loved ones and professionals.

I have written a lot of poetry/prose/rambles throughout this period to articulate my inner world to myself and I take it to privately paid therapy.

Brenda

I have been caring for my daughter since she was 18 years old. She's had problems since she was 15 and she was attending a CAMHS without my knowledge. She told me much later that she didn't want me to be upset! This was more than 19 years ago, and we had been expecting her to take up a place at university to read Sports Science; instead, I was called to see a psychiatrist who informed me that she was having suicidal thoughts and self-harming. This was when my role changed, and I became a carer as well as a mother. She was in hospital from April until November. I visited her most days, but she didn't seem to improve despite medication. During the first few weeks of hospitalisation, her friends visited, but as September came and they went off to university, she was left without visitors, apart from some family members. She became isolated and her social structure vanished; her fellow patients became her friends because of their shared experiences.

As a mother, it is sad to see the person you care for making no progress. At this time, I thought that she would get better and did not know a great deal about mental health problems. I didn't realise she was psychotic until I was taking her out and the nurse asked how her voices were. I was always anxious about how she would react in any given outing, and travelling by train, I worried she might jump on the line. This anxiety has never left me and even today, 19 years on, I am still anxious if I can't contact her. Allied to this is the guilt I can still feel. *How did I not realise that she was ill? Am I responsible for her illness?* Although, rationally, I know the answer, the guilt and anxiety remain. Compared to the start, my daughter has vastly improved; she has a boyfriend and social contacts outside of the family. She plays hockey in a club. She is about to start a course to become a mental health volunteer. This doesn't mean that my anxiety has gone, but it is good to know that at present this is as good as it gets. At the start of her illness, I knew very little about mental health problems and the treatments. It was a steep learning curve. Her diagnosis was changing all the time and with this, the powerful medications that she took. I use the Internet to keep up to date with the latest findings on psychosis and have taken some courses to help me. I find that one of the most important aspects in my role is to get as much knowledge about psychosis as I can and get support from carer groups.

Fhiona

At age 18, while attending art college, our son started experiencing music in his head all the time. The local psychiatrist reassured him and us that he was 'interesting and creative' and despite some bizarre behaviour, was perfectly well. As parents, we felt we needed more reassurance and within the week saw another psychiatrist who considered him an 'extremely disturbed young person' and admitted him to a young person's mental health unit with a diagnosis of schizophrenia. This was bewildering and frightening for us, but so much worse and scary for him. Our son started taking strong anti-psychotic medication at this point. After four months, and aged 19 years old, we were advised to send him to a mental health hostel for people with long-term problems. At this low point, our determination kicked in and we decided to avoid making him a permanent cog in the mental health system. However, we were unprepared for the uncertainty, worry and insecurity ahead, a rollercoaster of highs and lows.

Every person will have an individual response to any treatment, so our challenge was to understand this and get to know the 'new person'. After the professional input, we had to find ways of encouraging our son to stick with it, cheer him up and inspire him to keep going. Developing trust in the professional advice was a big thing for me, and even when there were glitches, gradually realising that most professionals try their best and do the best they can at the time. No one deliberately gives bad advice. Outings and meals out were helpful in learning how to cope. Getting to know others in recovery was also helpful.

Over the years, going through the rollercoaster process has been all consuming and tiring, and looking back I can now see there was a massive impact on all the family. Socially, our lives were curtailed and emotionally we had to understand the 'new person' changed by a cocktail of anti-psychotic drugs. For me, coping as a carer has meant carrying on, being persistent and not giving up. It has been about moving from a place of complete inexperience to an awareness of what is needed. It is important to look after oneself and have a hobby or interest to pursue . . . to be able to switch off. A support group provided an important base to any coping activity; it can almost be a haven. It is a place to learn, a place to share, a place to find courage and confidence, and a place to think about challenging the system. And very importantly, a place to welcome new people who are bewildered at the start of their journey.

David and Ann

The opening line from Tolstoy's *Anna Karenina* (1878) 'Happy families are all alike; every unhappy family is unhappy in its own way' captured how life felt 23 years ago when we wrote 'Who Cares?', about our experiences of supporting a daughter with a severe mental disorder and the NHS care she received. Thankfully, the rawness of that early experience no longer haunts us. And the asylum that was grooming Mary for a life of disability, aged just 18, no longer stands. Overcoming this awful start, took many years and is testament to Mary's resilience, our persistence as her advocates, and the dedication of some mental health practitioners who never gave up on her. Writing today about our experiences of caregiving lets us reflect on a long and gradual process of healing that has brought us to a very different place to the one we almost resigned ourselves to back then.

A downside of being health practitioners (David, a GP, Ann, a district nurse) was that we were trained to have an unduly pessimistic view for those given a diagnosis of schizophrenia – now appreciated to be more the result of institutional care in the old asylums than the nature of the disorder. And there was our daughter in just such a setting. Being effective caregivers for Mary hinged on us first addressing our own low expectations. In unlocking our pessimism, one person stood out – Mary's psychiatrist. She not only had the courage to urge us to complain about the service she was providing Mary, but she also had the wisdom and experience to help the complaint materialise into a new rehabilitation service based in the real world two years later.

Even though progress was often slow, with the support of Mary's psychiatrist and this new service we learnt how to travel hopefully, seize opportunities, and celebrate tiny gains that over time built into tangible improvement. This experience transformed the way we supported Mary. A mindset of hopeful expectation became one of the essential tools in our caregiver recovery toolkit – as relevant today as it was then.

What else found its way into our caregiver recovery toolkit? Tools for negotiating, navigating and advocating with services have been vital. But in describing these, we wonder what it would have been like had we not been experienced health practitioners.

1. Finding a suitable treatment in the first few years was critical to Mary improving, but brought with it the challenge of supporting her to monitor and manage the side effects. Twenty-five years on we are still actively **negotiating** these trade-offs with her psychiatric team, problem-solving practical ways to deal with difficult side effects, encouraging antipsychotic dose reductions while remaining vigilant for signs of the psychosis relapsing.
2. Long term impacts of her psychiatric condition and its treatment on her physical health have made things increasingly complicated. Although only in her mid-40s, Mary now experiences four additional physical conditions each with their own set of treatments, investigations and monitoring requirements. **Navigating** these through all the different practitioners and services, we have been the constant over the last 25 years by holding the narrative of who Mary is and how her increasingly complex medical history affects her.
3. Our caregiver toolkit would be incomplete without reflecting on how our **advocacy** has supported Mary on three critical occasions when decisions were being made about her by local health and social care commissioners. The first, to prevent Mary being sent over 50 miles from her home to receive rehabilitation, the second to stop a threatened abrupt withdrawal of social support without any prior discussion, and the third to highlight a residential care setting that became unsafe for Mary's increasingly complex needs. Mary has always benefitted from an excellent psychiatric team, and yet despite their multi-agency assessment cataloguing serious unmet need, each time our caregiver advocacy was essential to convince (polite version) commissioners to address these needs. And now to today. Twenty-five years on, our hopes and concerns as caregivers have changed. We find ourselves with some sense of personal peace from seeing Mary happy and fulfilled in a high-quality care home close-by, as we reach an age where our own health and mortality may impact on Mary, and her brothers and their families. How different we might have felt had Mary not moved to her present home three years ago – the previous home's inability to meet her basic daily living needs, culminating in a series of physical health crises. Nonetheless, a recent incident that we had to deal with shows how, as caregivers, we can never fully relax.

This theme of self-determination and empowerment has lain at the heart of our recovery. Leaving behind that "*family unhappy in its own way*" first required us to imagine a very different future to the one being offered by the bleak asylum. This was the critical turning point. Inspired by some key professionals, we began to construct a new set of expectations that ultimately influenced a very different personal and family narrative. Gone was the constant 'why us?' – our feelings of failure as parents – her two brothers bemused and hiding concerns that they might inherit what their sister had. In its place has grown a pride in how Mary has come through. Her warm and loving nature has restored. She is connected happily with us, her brothers and their families, and enjoys life with the extended family of her care home, grounded in the community we have all lived in for the last 40 years. Our whole family has regained its balance, and family life now feels reassuringly ordinary. Once more able to have fun and to be serious, to laugh and to cry, to work and to play . . . not perfect, just an ordinary life.

Amanda

Having kids can be the most amazing experience of our lives and a lot of fun when things are going well, but as much as we try to protect them, the unexpected can happen. What I never really thought about or expected, was that any of them may develop mental health issues, even though these, I later realised but had previously suspected, were present in my family. Perhaps having been brought up by a parent with, what I have more recently understood were undiagnosed mental health issues and possibly autism, I didn't initially identify the same issues in one of my children when they started to become apparent. I first noticed that my eldest son had similarities to my mother when he was still at primary school, but I had no idea what this would mean for his future development. Even as some of his behaviour as a teenager started to worry me, when I mentioned it to his father, he would try to make light of it, probably to put mine and his own mind at rest. At the time, I was mostly concerned about the effect it was having on our daughter, who was often the target of my son's paranoia and mood swings/aggression. It was very stressful for her as he would accuse her of breaking things in his room or moving his stuff or even knocking on his wall all night to keep him awake and annoy him. So as these imagined acts of sabotage increased in number and became more bizarre, so did his behaviour towards her become more aggressive and paranoid. I was stressed and still feel responsible as a parent that we didn't seem able to do much to improve things for my daughter regarding my son's behavior at that time and that we weren't aware of the extent of the damage also inflicted on our other children by his mental illness.

Our marriage and my husband's relationship with our son deteriorated. I don't think we were aware of how much stress we were under. The marriage started to break down and we first separated and later divorced. It was such a stressful time, it was just awful, but I couldn't carry on with what the relationship was doing to the children and to me, probably also to my husband. I think if we had had some help earlier or pursued therapy, we may still be together, or it would have helped us. We never had a break or any respite from our situation which was often so fun and a wonderful experience but could also become unmanageably stressful. It was in the second year of university that my son had his first psychotic breakdown and returned home.

I was doing too much really and trying to keep it all together. Sport really helped me unwind, but it was an extra thing I had to organise myself to get around to doing. I sometimes competed at events locally and elsewhere. Training helped focus me as I put all my excess energy and perhaps anxiety into my sporting activities, but now I don't know how I did it all. I suppose that we all manage stress and anxiety in different ways and at the time, it was my outlet. Family life and being a single working mother was manageable until my son attacked one of his siblings and the police got involved. This was the start of a gradual downward spiral in terms of my son's mental health and there was more police involvement as his behaviours became public and increasingly unmanageable. Following several years of trying to get help, he received a schizophrenia and Asperger's diagnoses.

My son was sectioned several times for years, with disappearances and frequent attempts to escape from the mental health care institution he was at. On one occasion when he was missing for a few days, we didn't know whether he was even still alive. During those days, I couldn't really cope, and I started using alcohol to numb myself and tried to sleep but couldn't. I had also suffered a head injury during sports training with months of post-concussion syndrome, total amnesia before and after the accident for several weeks, and difficulty coping with my full-time job and daily family life. This was also around the time I was prescribed anti-depressants and I started drinking more frequently, which helped fuel my need to block out any pain and accept what was happening with my son. It wasn't a very helpful thing at all, and I do wish I had been able to care for myself more in the same way I had cared and still cared for my kids. I asked to come off the anti-depressants, but I unfortunately did still used to drink when I became distressed by any deterioration in my son's mental health, or every time he went missing or whenever there was an incident of any kind. It was the only way to sleep really. I was also prescribed sleeping pills. Although I was still involved with sport, I stopped competing, as I just wasn't able to focus on anything.

I was working full time and still trying to keep up a semblance of a normal life with my other children who had their own issues and challenges in life. It was very difficult to accept, especially for myself and the rest of the family, that this brilliant, funny genius and athlete had lost everything he had achieved and was experiencing a constant living nightmare in his mind, which was his new reality. As his personality changed, the gifted person we knew gradually disappeared. The only thing that kept me sane and made me stronger was the fact that I had other wonderful children who needed me, and the gradually diminishing hope that he would improve or could go back to what he was.

I had to stay strong for my kids throughout several years of trying to achieve a better outcome for my son, which I eventually achieved by putting in writing to a health minister. After eight years of what felt like a constant struggle and battle to improve things for my son, he was transferred to a specialist unit. I was so happy for him, and this gave me renewed hope, but I didn't expect to have what people describe as a nervous breakdown the day after he left. I think I just could no longer deal with the pain and had previously done everything I could to shut it off, and I had been doing that for too long.

I had some therapy in the past as a teenager luckily, but I also resumed therapy more recently and it has helped me in spite of my avoidant tendencies. The psychotherapist helped me identify some distress patterns in my life and unresolved trauma, but my therapy sessions ended soon after as I was working long hours and found it more and more difficult to attend the sessions, partly because I didn't really like talking about my son or other family members as it felt like it made things worse, probably because I tended to block any feelings about it all in order to be able to cope. I just wanted my son to get better, to go back to being the person he had been, and not constantly tortured by his own mind. I have recognised I do still have outstanding issues to address, and I have a tendency to take on too much until it suddenly all gets too much, so I try to limit myself now so that I can focus better and stick at things for longer.

I hoped for a long time that my son would 'improve' or 'get better', but what many people aren't really aware of and, in my case, find it very difficult to accept or perhaps come to terms with, is that schizophrenia is a lifelong condition. I hope we were loving parents for our son. We did our best, that's all we can do as parents, and we have to stop blaming ourselves and feeling guilty as parents always do. We always think, 'what could we/I have done better? Did it happen partly due to this or that, what if . . .?' It is good to explore this up to a point or try to understand potential catalysts or how things could have been different had we realised this or that, but totally blaming ourselves as parents doesn't really help anyone; and even though I do believe my son should have been protected from some potential stress factors, we can't protect our children from life and the realities that presents. He may have developed his condition whatever his external circumstances, he may not have done; his presentation may have been more or less severe, but we will never know.

Being told our child has schizophrenia must be one of the most difficult things to experience and accept; it is like experiencing a loss, a bereavement of sorts. We do partially or sometimes totally lose the person they once were, that we imagined they would become. But, as we all know, life delivers no promises and perhaps we don't really lose things, as everything evolves, and everything is a part of an ongoing process of change. We do need to grieve properly, but first we need to try to accept. In acceptance, positive action, love and self-love, there is hope, growth, knowledge and the potential to explore and develop ourselves as human beings and find a strength we never thought we had and, through that, maybe even help others.

I would like to end this on a hopeful note as I know how difficult this particular journey can be for all involved, and I still am trying to heal myself and accept some help. I do find it very healing to spend time with my son and know that I have improved his day or week in some way. Previously, it was mostly via video chat but now he is back, I am fortunate enough to be able to have some input. I realise that this isn't and may never be the case for so many. I know what this condition can do. I believe we do have to become stronger than we ever thought we could become, and we can then perhaps even evolve and help others. This also is hope and self-love. We have been and are still going through a very painful process and we have done amazingly well to be contributing to, or reading, this book.

3 PARTNER CAREGIVER ACCOUNTS

Olumuyiwa

I am an informal carer for my partner, and I have been playing this role for several years. I also have a daughter aged six years old. Being a carer has been challenging due to managing the different role and responsibilities as a partner, carer, and a father.

Initially, I had no idea or knowledge about my partner's diagnosis, which made it difficult for me to understand how to manage her care. I requested a meeting with her community psychiatric nurse, which I attended, along with my partner. The nurse was able to educate me about the diagnosis, the illness, and ways to support her treatment. The meeting helped me in such a significant way because I felt that I was able to understand my partner's difficulties, what I could do to help, and sources of support if I needed it. Soon after, I registered with a carer support service, where I was able to learn more about how to manage my partner's illness. I feel that my engagement with the mental health services helped me in my carer role for my partner. I have been able to monitor the medication she has, including understanding their side-effects, and look out for signs of a relapse. I have been involved in her care and treatment plans.

It is important to recognise that the relationship that I have with my partner encourages me to ensure her wellbeing and that of our family. But making sure my partner's health is in a stable condition and that my daughter enjoys a perfect family home, does not come without a price. In prioritising the needs of my family, I have not been able to find a suitable job that can fit in or work around my carer responsibilities. I am not being paid as a carer and I do not have recourse to any public funds. This makes the situation rather difficult, financially, as I must rely on my partner's benefits to get by. Not feeling able to financially provide for my family has led to stress within our family. But the assistance of services through facilitating referrals to family therapy and carers' groups have really helped me with how to manage situations through more communication, to share my experiences with other carers, and to strike a balance between my roles as a carer, a partner and father. The boundaries and the issues faced by those caring for a partner are different from those faced by other carers. Talking to other carers and having therapy helped me manage those boundaries. I feel I can distinguish between my carer and partner roles. Having good communication with the services has allowed me to have more better understanding of my partner's care.

Chidem

I have loved my husband since I was 18 years old, and when we eventually got together some years later, as a couple, we talked about his mental health problems, which I thought was, and understood to be, depression, but it was so much more. I have been caring for 30 years for my husband who lives with schizophrenia, and we have a beautiful grown-up son. It has not been an easy ride for anyone.

What a carer does is so big, it is hard for me to put into words. I gave up my whole life to care for my husband. Over time, my life gradually became his life, and I eventually stopped having my mine. Mental illness is still a hard thing to understand for most people. It took me years and years to understand my husband's illness. In the beginning, it was a big struggle not knowing much about the illness, but working in a pharmacy helped me to get some understanding about the medications. However, living with the illness at home was something very different. Schizophrenia has been torturous for my husband, and the treatments he received were not any better; some have been horrendous.

Over the years, my caring role has made me stronger, particularly when the illness is so up and down. To help me cope and get through, I have had to separate the illness from my husband and approach them differently and remind myself that they were different things. When unwell, my husband is a totally different person from the one that I know and love. When he is well, he is an angel; a kind, gentle, and decent person, and that is why I am here and have been for all these years. If he had been a nasty person, someone that was abusive, then I would not have looked after him.

Caring does take it out of you, and you must think about yourself. I had been caring for so long that it became obvious that if I did not start to look after myself, then I would no longer be able to look after him. I thought to myself, 'right, you know what, if you're going to survive this then you will have to be hard'. So now, as soon as I see my husband going downhill, I don't hesitate, I will contact the mental health team and let them know and work with them to make things better. It has been very hard for me and there were periods when I just became very anxious and emotional because it just hurt. Sometimes, I wanted to say that I can't take this anymore, but then I found a way to carry on.

When you're caring, you can always feel alone. You know there are thousands of other people with similar stories, but you do feel alone and isolated. At this time of the year (Christmas), it can be even harder when I see how other people are getting on and buying presents and so on, but I just learned to live with it and carry on. Having support from other carers is important to me. In a carers' group that I am part of, there are other mothers, fathers, siblings, and partners and many others that attend. It can be hard to talk about what you are dealing with, but I have been dealing with the illness for so long now that I have an 'I don't care' attitude. Having the chance to speak to like-minded people, who understand me and what I experience, and have gone through similar things, is key. It has made me stronger talking to other carers and listening to them. They can also take ideas from me too because of what I have been through and seen over the years.

I look at things differently because of my caring role, and, over the years, it has not been all doom and gloom; there have been times when he has been well. I am a very stubborn and determined person. I always believe that things can get better, and they usually do. During hard times, I tell myself that "I will get through this and tomorrow will be another day". I make a point of not dwelling on the past. I always look forward to another day and do not look back. When my husband has been admitted to hospital for treatment, I tell myself that he will get better and will come out.

I am quite resilient and would not have been able to survive over the years if I was not mentally stubborn. In my caring role, I have been through the worst when I did not know anything about the illness. As a carer, you should never be afraid or ashamed to talk, and if you want to be emotional and cry, then do it. It will be best to let things out. Being a carer takes over your life, so honesty is important and letting others know if you are struggling.

4 SIBLING CAREGIVER ACCOUNTS

Chinyere

My brother was different right from childhood. A lot of firsts in the family were witnessed in him. The age gap between him and his immediate younger sibling was the shortest (less than two years). He stood and walked later than his five siblings and he was the only one to have a febrile seizure. However, my brother was also more sociable than anyone else in our family; the only one interested in the entertainment industry. As a child, sometimes he would manifest some baffling behaviours that our straitlaced family found difficult to understand. This led to punishments in an effort to curb some of these behaviours. I think because he was punished more often than the well-behaved siblings, perhaps he had a feeling of not being loved as much as they were.

During adolescence he began to drink, smoke cigarettes and cannabis, stay out late at night, without permission, pilfer money and hang around with people that our family found unsavoury. My parents could not understand where these behaviours were coming from. They tried several punitive measures, including physical chastising and grounding, all in the hope of extinguishing some of these behaviours that were perceived out of the ordinary for our family, our community and our culture. But these failed.

My brother had his first episode of psychosis at the age of 22, approximately 20 years ago. It was during his final year, while writing his final set of examinations as an undergraduate at university. I think his attempts to cram four years' of work in a few weeks might have played a role. Initially, no one could understand why he was talking excessively or becoming angry over minor issues and claiming that his ideas had been stolen by big industry entertainment giants. He was diagnosed with schizoaffective disorder. With medications he got well after a few weeks but refused to continue with treatment because of weight gain. Subsequently, he relapsed, and this became a familiar pattern. Thus, whenever he got a job and things did not succeed as fast as he would have liked them to, or his excessively lofty and poorly thought-out plans failed, he would experience a relapse. The relapses have been countless; in the last 20 years, he has been well for a total of three years.

Over the years, I feel that my brother has lost out on several opportunities because of his decision to decline treatments. He described having many difficulties associated with medications, including weakness, drowsiness, erectile dysfunction and excessive weight gain. He insisted that he would rather die than take them. According to my brother, medications were contrived to make him weak so that he would not embarrass our family. Attempts with counselling also failed. He has turned down offers to see a clinical psychologist or a psychiatrist and prefers to visit spiritualists because he believes that he has been cursed and required deliverance not medications. Thus, my brother's compliance with treatments has been poor; most treatments he has received have been brief, forceful, and given when we no longer feel able to cope with embarrassing and, at times, dangerous behaviours. Several attempts at rehabilitation have failed; he often runs away from treatment centres or is ejected for inciting revolt among the patients. He refuses follow up care but when he is relapsing, he can become excessively jealous of anyone getting close to our parents, which often leaves my parents becoming isolated, just like my brother is. Though my brother has been able to write some novels, his earnings have been poor. He is unable to hold down a job, which has invariably left him financially and emotionally dependant on the family.

I think the illness has robbed my parents of joy. My mother says that this illness has made it difficult to appreciate the achievements of her other children. After studying medicine, I chose to specialise in psychiatry with the aim of helping my brother with his illness. This was not successful because it is difficult trying to help someone who does not want to be helped. For several years now, I get nervous whenever my phone rings and I see that it is a call from home. I worry about the possible genetic basis of the disorder. I get nervous about visiting my parents whenever he relapses because of the unpredictability of his actions. My siblings and I get nervous for our parents because of how he isolates them, and people are reluctant to visit.

About two years ago, my parents took him away from the family home to a religious setting, as they could no longer manage his behaviour. He was away from home for nearly two years but eventually ran away from there. He was then taken to a psychiatric hospital where he was admitted for about four months. I am unsure what happened but have wondered whether his experiences, over the past two years, have shown him the difficulties that you can have when the family are not around to give support and protect him. I also think that maybe he has become more mature with age but, either way, he no longer misses his hospital appointments, he is compliant with his medications and rehabilitation is ongoing. Currently, because of his somewhat improved compliance with treatment, the atmosphere at home has been a lot more relaxed. Over the years, I have had my children and my job to keep me busy and I try to keep my mind away from him. Though one cannot but regret a life that has been wasted, you then convince yourself that you have done as much as you can for him.

Abi

My younger brother has a diagnosis of schizophrenia, and we are close in age. I'm 28, he is 25. We had a wonderful childhood, hung out in the same social circles, and got along well. I never noticed anything was different, he was just always a sensitive and kind person. When he became unwell, it was difficult to know how to help him at first. Our family dynamics changed, and our relationship took a hit when communication broke down. His mental health problems have not only changed who I am but have changed the way I live my life.

My brother was referred to a specialist service that dealt with people who experience first episodes of psychosis. Myself and my family also received support during this time. I now work for the team who helped my brother, employed as a peer support worker. I use my experience of caring for my brother to try and help individuals experiencing psychosis and their families, especially siblings who may be overlooked as carers.

Before working for the service, I worked on my own challenges that surfaced as a result of feeling confused and useless watching my brother experience distressing symptoms and multiple admissions to hospital. I had to discover my own tools for coping and healing so that I could be the best person I could be for him. I started creating art regularly again, painting, drawing, and documenting my experiences. This was a great relief to return to my passion. I had previously studied Fine Art at university but neglected this part of myself when I struggled to cope with my brother's illness and the tension at home. I now recognise the importance of keeping up one's interests and hobbies during stressful periods. I often introduce and explore the idea of visual expression with clients and siblings I meet, and supply art packs and sessions to support others relieve pressures and feelings of isolation.

Six years since the initial referral, we are much more hopeful for my brother's future. and are supporting him to develop the skills he needs to become independent. Right now, he still lives with my parents, and I visit a couple times a week to hang out and just be there as his sister. The experiences have changed us as a family, but we have become much closer as a result.

Maggie

Three years older than me and, even from a young age, a scientific and mathematic genius, my brother was always socially awkward. Although undiagnosed, both he and I have talked about and suspect he may well have high-functioning autism. Yin and Yang, we are complementary, inter-connected and interdependent. We share a puerile sense of humour, an intense bond, and parents. My brother and I looked after and out for each other. He is unbelievably generous, painfully honest, hilarious, intelligent, extremely handsome, and the most honourable and fair person I know – frustratingly, he doesn't see any of this. At the age of 45, he left his wife, met a new partner, told me he was truly in love for the first time in his life, started taking recreational drugs (having never so much as smoked a cigarette in his youth) and was happier and more confident than he'd ever been. He then went through an incredibly stressful and protracted divorce that put him in debt.

Not long after he was blindsided by the divorce settlement news, his new partner called me. She said she was extremely concerned about him. My brother became more and more withdrawn from her and from me. And this is where things become a little hazy. Where narratives blur and tangle. My brother's take on what was happening, and his partner's account were completely different. When their stories were completely divergent I, of course, knew who to trust. My brother. The person who I knew to be the most honest, dependable and logical person I know! Her account was that following an affair she'd had, he'd become paranoid and had started secretly filming her. He said she was continuing to be unfaithful and, because the affair was with her brother-in-law, she was now so scared of the truth coming out that she was trying to discredit his version of events by telling everyone he was suffering from psychosis. She told me not to believe anything he said and that he was hooked on methamphetamine, and she was leaving him. Crystal Meth!! This, I felt, knowing my brother, even with her introducing him to recreational drugs, was highly implausible. My brother's behaviour, at this point, was entirely within what was normal for him. To an impartial observer, it may be much more obvious that someone is clearly suffering from psychotic delusions. Someone impartial doesn't have prior history, they don't factor in that the person you know better than anyone else in the world, is intensely logical, extremely scientific and incapable of lying. When they tell you something is categorically true, you have no reason not to believe them; in fact, you have every reason to believe them. In the foothill of psychosis, the delusions can be entirely plausible, based on reality and backed up by entirely rational explanation.

My brother took a forensic approach to proving to me, but mainly to himself, that this wasn't and couldn't possibly be psychosis. An approach that anyone else might consider to be evidence of a departure from reality, but, to me, was just the normal way my brother would approach this challenge. If you believe you can hear people talking to you but someone else is denying this, then the obvious course of action is to audio record; transcribe what you can hear then write a computer programme that splits that audio into tiny component parts, randomly scrambles them, listen to the de-constructed audio, transcribe that and then reassemble the transcript and see if it matches your original transcription! Of course, you do! For hours and hours, for days, for weeks, for months, until you've proved to yourself that you haven't imagined this, it's scientifically impossible and therefore real. He did this at the expense of sleeping or eating but, I later found out, with the help of a lot of alcohol and drugs to keep him awake and alert from what he perceived to be threats and danger.

At this point, my brother was living alone in London, and me and my husband were nearly 800 miles away in the South of France. He felt as though he had lost everything, and now he told me that he categorically knew that his girlfriend was not just having an affair and planning to leave him, but she was also planning to empty his bank account and kill him. He was obsessively listening to the audio he'd made to try and work out why, what had happened and what had made her hate him this much. He was also now convinced that she had bugged the flat and was listening to him, watching him and communicating with him to make everyone think he was delusional and psychotic. Every night he would send me long text messages detailing everything he could now hear, initially through his bugged mobile, then through speakers, then from all and any electronic devices in the flat, and finally through the walls.

Of course, now, it was clear to me that he was suffering from all the classic signs of psychosis. He had auditory hallucinations that were rapidly becoming more and more persecutory and florid. More and more characters were becoming involved, and 'they' were all threatening him in an increasingly complex plot. I offered to come and stay with him for a while, but he believed it would be unsafe for me to come and put myself at risk. I tried to protest that I had no concerns about my safety, but I just didn't want him to be dealing with this alone. I felt so utterly bereft. I was unbelievably concerned for his wellbeing but also felt that I had no option but to respect his wish, as an adult, that he did not want me to come and help him. I felt all I could do was to keep the communication channel open and do all I could to support him as best I could, and as much as he would allow.

The only other thing I felt I could do, at that stage, was to find out as much as I possibly could about psychosis – *what it was, symptoms, triggers, treatments, prognosis, recovery*. I could find loads of information, but the stuff that really helped in my understanding took a lot of searching for. Some useful stuff is deeply buried in research papers and written in inaccessible clinical terminology. From what I read, I was impressed by early intervention and by Open Dialogue approaches and deeply concerned about the effects of sectioning and medication. I was acutely aware that the earlier he got support, the better the prognosis, but felt as though my only option, at that point, was to try and get him to realise he needed support himself. When I asked him if he had any thoughts of self-harm, he was clear that he was doing all he could to keep himself safe from the harm of others and had no intentions at all of self-harm. He is gentle, has never been violent and has never so much as threatened anyone ever. So, whenever I reached out to talk to mental health services about what I could do, they would ask if he was in danger of harming others or himself, and I didn't feel he was.

I tried the tactic of simply suggesting to him that he was understandably dealing with a lot of stress and possibly suffering from depression, and urged him to see his GP, but whilst he agreed that he was depressed, he was convinced that the GP would just not believe what was really going on and would think he had psychosis and have him sectioned, and that's what 'they' wanted. Any remotely gentle forages of conversations where I asked him to consider or be open minded about what was going on made him stressed and close down. His life became more and more difficult. He was locking himself into his flat with all the curtains closed and sometimes locking himself into one room believing that 'they' weren't just coming for him, 'they' were in the flat, just outside the door or pouring gas in through the letterbox. He was arming himself with whatever he could find to defend himself from attack. I would talk to him as calmly as possible and, without challenging his beliefs, try and come up with alternative explanations for him to consider. I tried to appeal to his scientific nature. We talked about the phenomenon of apophenia and the brain's tendency to look for patterns and find meaning in random things. He completely understood this; he'd been to a lecture many years earlier all about apophenia but, he said, this was absolutely not what was happening in this case, this was different, this was real.

At this stage, I became increasingly desperate but completely at a loss as to what to do. I felt as though his mental health was rapidly deteriorating, but I knew I could only get him more help by forcing him, against his will, to be assessed and, in doing so, potentially jeopardising his one lifeline to the only person he trusted. Every suggestion I made that could lead him to see for himself that he needed help was rejected, and I was in constant fear of pushing him too far. I did what I could on a practical level: sent him food deliveries; I urged him to contact me day or night whenever he needed to. Me and my husband abandoned our lives in France so I could be nearer to my brother just in case he would let me see him. I did an online course to find out more about the links between psychosis, stress and autism; I read extensively. I desperately searched for stories of other carers' experiences and successful tactics for supporting someone with psychosis who doesn't see that they need help, but these were really hard to find.

I read a lot about the negative implications of long-term use of anti-psychotics, and I kept thinking how stressful being sectioned would be and how that seemed like the worst-case scenario. I kept thinking that if only I could find some way to persuade him to come and live with us, in a calm environment where I could reduce his stress and support him to access early intervention services and talking therapies, I could help him to recover without him being sectioned or put on medications for years. I tried so many tactics to try and get him to realise that coming to live with us (me and my husband) or allowing me to come and live with him was the best way of him keeping safe (he thought I meant from 'them' and I, of course I meant, from the illness). Somehow or other, I managed never to lie directly to my brother or to validate his beliefs, but I tied myself in linguistic knots to tread this line. I managed to talk about psychosis in the third person. To talk about what happens to other people who suffered from stressed or drug-induced psychosis. He was interested in it, as a topic, and whilst categorically denying that he had psychosis, this became a way of being able to at least talk about stress and the potential effects of this on the brain.

But then something dramatic happened. He told me that he had been sat with his head in his hands and 'they' were watching him, and he heard 'them' say that 'they' didn't need to kill him because he was going to kill himself. I asked him if this was right, and if he was thinking of killing himself and he categorically denied this. He told me that 'they' were mistaken, 'they' had misread his body language but that he could now fool 'them' into thinking whatever he wanted. However, I heard something very different and extremely worrying. Much of what he told me the persecutory voices were saying seemed to me to be his own deep-seated fears, his feelings about himself, his worries and anxieties. I'd felt as though my role was to be the counter to this, to remind him of everything that was brilliant about him in the hope that might filter through. Him telling me that 'they' thought he was going to kill himself was a clear indicator to me of his own suicidal ideation. I knew then that I had no option than to force him to have help. I spoke to his GP, and this felt horrendous; to go behind his back and to intervene without his knowledge. I felt I couldn't be honest with him and tell him what I was doing as that could mean he would sever all contact and be completely alone with this. If I'm brutally honest, and with the gift of hindsight, I feared for him being alone, but I also feared for me losing my relationship with him forever. At this point, those felt almost of equal concern – and thinking about that now just makes me feel as though this was me being selfish. Caring about my relationship with him over his ultimate wellbeing.

His GP suggested I contact mental health services and ask for him to be assessed. When my brother told me that mental health services had rocked up unannounced and assessed him, he believed that his ex-girlfriend had made this happen and just added this into the evidence that everything he believed was true – she and 'those' working with her had the power to get him sectioned! I told him that I thought it was more likely that the police (who he had called out on a number of occasions) had requested this assessment as they, like I, were concerned for him and wanting to eliminate the possibility that any of what he was experiencing was because of stress rather than genuine threats from third parties. My brother was detained under Section 3. Initially this felt like an enormous relief. I felt as though he would be safe, he would be cared for, he would recover and that he would realise how ill he was and that the threats he perceived were not real. However, my relief was almost instantly replaced by feelings of overwhelming guilt and, far from the fear for his safety dissipating, it increased. He was absolutely outraged to be detained against his will. He couldn't believe that his liberty could be taken away like this. He felt that 'they' had won. 'They' had wanted him to be perceived as being psychotic and 'they' had managed to convince everyone that he was.

When I spoke to him, he was so depressed and that felt even more unsettling for me. I remember him telling me that, through the slits in the metal screens on the window, he could just see the end of a rainbow and he said, 'I'm never going to see the whole of a rainbow ever again'. It was absolutely devastating. I just wanted to save him from this. After a week, under threat of force if he didn't comply, my brother started to take anti-psychotics. He was terrified these would just turn him into a zombie, make him unable to work. The fact that the drugs made him sleep most of the day, kept him awake with restless legs most of the night, and he rapidly gained weight, helped reinforce this fear. Due to COVID, there was no visiting, but I could phone the ward and I could phone my brother – he was allowed his mobile. I felt there was so little I could say to console him – all I could do was listen. I fell back on the humour we shared. At times it worked to pull him out of his deep pit of desperation, but it worked less and less as he became more depressed. I phoned him every day, but I even started to dread the call, worrying about what I could say to help, how I could support him without agreeing with whatever he believed. I managed to hold it together for every conversation and try and listen, be empathetic, be upbeat, joke if I could. But every time I put the phone down, I'd just cry, sometimes for hours and sometimes all through the night. I had a feeling of absolute inconsolable hopelessness, like bereavement. What made it worse was feeling so responsible; like so many relatives, I felt that I was responsible for him being there. I thought I'd done the right thing, the only thing I could do, but ended up feeling as though this experience could be the catalyst in itself to him spiralling downward and never being able to 'see the rainbow' again! I started to imagine him taking his own life and it being my fault. I literally found myself repeatedly thinking through getting a call to tell me he'd committed suicide, and me planning his funeral. I'd write his eulogy endlessly in my head.

I wasn't sleeping, and lying awake one night I found a large lump in my stomach which turned out to be a big tumour on my ovary; my blood results showed raised markers and after scans and an emergency operation, I ended up with a stoma. But this gets just two lines in my whole account because, as horrendous as that was, it was a mere footnote to dealing with my brother's psychosis. This is what makes you realise how all-consuming dealing with a loved one with psychosis is. You feel so utterly desperate and so alone; it's pretty much all you think about every waking hour, and you have a lot of waking hours. You have no bandwidth left for anything else, your life, your health. Friends and relations all have their own opinions on what you should do – all incredibly well-meaning and most trying to get you to take care of yourself, seeing how much stress you are under and how dangerously close to becoming mentally unwell yourself.

Some were, strangely, unempathetic about my brother's plight, feeling that he'd bought this on himself, through his life choices. They pointed out to me that he was an adult and, whilst he was my brother, he was not my responsibility. Again, I think, well-meaning and trying to protect me from overwhelming feelings of guilt, but they just felt like additional stress. Some friends were brilliant, offering practical support, insight, unconditional love and understanding, but I started to feel as though I was just circling round and round in despair. You have no choice but to be the best advocate you can be to help navigate mental health services, to try and work out what you think is best and to do everything you can to make that happen. You feel as though you are the only person who really cares and who really knows the person who is now being seen just as a 'patient'. You feel desperate to tell those looking after him how lovely he is, how gentle he is, how loved he is.

The first time I was invited to phone in to join a hospital meeting about my brother, using a number and pin provided, I was in someone else's review meeting. The one and only time I got to 'join' I found, to my utter surprise, that I shared some of my brother's frustrations. There was little time, very little empathy, a lot of confronting and challenging his beliefs, which felt quite argumentative, with my brother getting stressed and frustrated. I struggled to see how progress would ever be made like this. This seemed to be counter to everything I'd read. The sole objective seemed to be to get my brother to say he recognised he had psychosis, and he was so far away from recognising this at all.

The worst Christmas and New Year ever came and went. He clearly needed help and was being given medication, but, beyond this, no useful interventions, no talking therapy and was just being held in an intensely stressful, tense and, at times, scary environment. On this basis, I told the responsible clinician that I believed it would be best for him to be discharged to come and live with me and my husband. I said that we would ensure he accessed community mental health support where we lived. I genuinely felt, at that stage, I could provide a better and safer environment for my brother to get well. They agreed to lift the section and I was invited to come and pick him up. I was invited in to join the discharge meeting. He was still suffering from psychosis, still convinced that 'they' would be waiting for him and me outside the unit to kill us. I'd hoped, in that meeting, to learn some amazing strategies of how to talk to my brother but instead I found myself mediating between my brother and staff and felt, to be honest, wholly unimpressed, and even more determined that getting him out of there was the best thing to do, however unwell he still was. So off we went, with my brother intensely agitated that 'they' would know he was being released and may well be there waiting for us. He could still 'hear', through his mobile that he believed was bugged, 'them' talking about their plans to kill and torture us and I started to realise what I was taking on. However, having this responsibility already felt so much better than feeling I had no agency at all.

My brother lived with me and my husband for five months. Initially, I think he was just so relieved to be out of the secure unit and have his own bedroom, office and bathroom, meals with us, and just to sleep properly. His fear was low level, he didn't feel he or we were at risk at our house and the narrative about 'them' flexed to justify this new feeling of security. We had visits from the Crisis Team and although my brother was a little reluctant to engage, he was clearly relieved that the approach they took was very different from the staff in the secure unit. They had more time, they listened to the entire background, they reassured him that 'IF' this was psychosis (and they always held back from saying it 100 per cent was) then there was nearly always a basis of truth. This open-minded stance made my brother willing to talk and willing to question things for himself. It made him calmer and more open and more willing to discuss. He was referred to an early intervention service.

He seemed to be getting better every day and, at these points, I loved having him with us. I loved the feeling that I could help him. I just loved having a closeness that we hadn't had a chance to have for years. I took time off work, we watched cartoons, went shopping for all the bad snacks that the drugs made him crave, and we basically regressed, together, to our childhood. I don't think this made things easy for my husband who later described this whole period as feeling as though I was having an affair with someone. I was entirely focused on my brother at the expense of every other relationship, including my marriage. After two weeks, he decided, as much as he was grateful for us offering him a place to live for a while, he wanted to go back 'home' to his flat in London. I told him I thought this was too soon and that I thought it would be better for him to stay with us for longer to really 'recover' from such an ordeal, but he was absolutely adamant. He went away for two weeks, saw his girlfriend who came to stay with him, and within days he was back into the most florid psychosis. He'd clearly stopped taking his anti-psychotics and had, instead, started taking drugs. I had calls again from the police and ambulance services and went to get him to come back to live with us.

At this point, he was the most unwell I'd ever seen. He was so terrified at points that it was difficult to not start becoming anxious and questioning reality yourself. The world truly looks like a different place through the lens of fear. To try and calm him or reassure him, I'd be up all night with him. I felt increasingly fragile myself, I couldn't work, and some family members were starting to suggest that my brother needed to be sectioned again and I strongly felt I just couldn't allow that. I found that my brother had been taking methamphetamine, something that I'd dismissed so long ago but now I could smell it in the house and found it just lying on his bed in his room. I tried to talk to him about it in a way that wouldn't make him just close down and lie to me. I just suggested that I didn't think that it would be helping and that it probably wasn't the greatest choice of drug, even when life is good. I felt so naïve, having always believed my brother that he was incapable of lying, but drugs and drug addiction changes can clearly make the most previously trustworthy person manipulative. My husband was not happy at all that my brother had been taking drugs in the house and it took all my powers of persuasion to convince him that the best course of action was to let my brother stay and for me and us to try and help him beat this addiction. I really couldn't think of any alternative at all anyway. I even started thinking that if I had to leave my house and my husband to keep my brother well, then that's what I'd have to do.

There were times when my brother was so convinced that 'they' were coming to kill us all that he just ran out of the house. There were times when I drove around trying to find him and, because of his state of agitation when he left, I found myself automatically driving to bridges and cliff tops as if my sub-conscious was more aware than my conscious self was that he was suicidal. I was so convinced he might take his own life, just by running from the fear that he felt. At this point, you start to feel as though you are taking care of someone you don't really know or recognise. I started to consider the idea that I couldn't help my brother to get well and that he might spiral downwards and take his own life, despite anything I could say or do. My brother became more insistent that I had to believe his delusions in order to keep us all safe. He started demanding that we do what he said to protect ourselves, and this was a line that neither me or my husband would cross. We'd do anything to try and reassure and calm but not change the way we lived our lives. My husband and I were arguing; I was crying myself to sleep, when

I could sleep at all. There were a few nights when my husband just took control and was far more controlling and insistent with my brother and I felt as though he was better equipped and more resilient to cope with my brother at that point.

My brother was, I knew, lying to me about taking the anti-psychotics but was angry if I just asked him about this. He did, however, seem adamant that he wanted me to help him kick the drugs and somehow or other he did manage this. As the psychosis lifted, my brother talked in a more open-minded way that some or all of what he'd experienced may have been psychosis. He said he now knew how to 'test' the voices to see if they were real or not. He asked them questions in his head, rather than out loud; if they answered, which they always did, he knew there were not real. He said the voices changed from coming from devices (phones, plug sockets, laptops) to just being around him and this made him know they were not real. They also changed from being persecutory to being complimentary, to building him up and making him feel more confident. All of the positive things that he reported 'them' saying were actually all of the things I'd said to him every day, believing that it really wasn't going in. 'You're a good-looking guy, you're funny, you're intelligent, you should feel so much better about yourself than you do'. Oh my God! This was an amazing turning point. I wasn't at all upset that he didn't attribute those things to me; much more powerfully, the things I'd said had somehow become his own inner voice. Wow! Just Wow! And there we were, so close to the lowest point, suddenly being in a good place. One I was intensely wary of, thinking it could shift at any moment and just be a brief respite between episodes.

But that was six months ago and, right now, there has been no further episodes. My brother is back in full-time work, back in a new flat in London, back with his ex-girlfriend and back in love. I'd love him to be able to talk about what happened, perhaps to reassure me that he has really recovered and that he has insight into what was going on, but he behaves as though none of this ever happened. There are legacies though, good and bad. On the positive front, he's more in touch with me that he was before and, without explicitly saying this, I feel as though this is his way of acknowledging what we went through together and that, as always, we were there for each other and always will be. On the negative side, it took an enormous toll on me. I suffered, for the first time in my life, from depression, I had insomnia for months, I told my husband I didn't love him, and I thought we should separate, and I spent weeks unable to work and unable to see a way forward. My behaviour was enormously self-destructive. I felt as though I started to process my own illness and cancer scare and operation in retrospect, like a weird PTSD, having not had the ability to deal with it at the time it was happening.

And now ... well, my husband gave me space and choice and consistently told me how much he loved me. I found that I needed anti-depressants for a short time myself, but gradually I'm returning to being me. I'm starting to feel the old mental resilience returning and I'm starting to feel loved and to love myself a little more again. The biggest positive is that not working for a while made me really question what I wanted to do and, like many psychosis carers I suspect, I thought I wanted to retrain as a mental health nurse or a social worker in mental health. Friends cautioned that this might just be a 'knee-jerk' reaction to what had happened and to give it some time before making a decision to re-train for three years and embark on a stressful career. Now, I've decided to use the background I do have, in digital developments, to develop online resources for families, friends and users of psychosis services.

I've realised, in writing this, how impossible it was for me to share my experience of psychosis, as a sibling carer, without providing every detail, every nuanced twist and turn, from start to current (is there ever a 'finish'?). Partly because the process of writing the entire story is so cathartic. But also, more strangely, because it feels like a luxury to be genuinely asked 'how was it for you?'. How was it for me? Well, it was singularly the most horrific experience of my life, bizarrely dappled with the most intensely wonderful moments as well. Moments that weren't in spite of my brother's psychosis but because of it. The experience of psychosis is such a complex labyrinth of narrative woven from truth, fears, external stimuli, inner thoughts, fragments of memories – deconstructed, scrambled and re-mixed to be presented back to a stressed and drug-addled mind as indistinguishable from reality. The detail in the narrative is clearly what makes everyone's (psychosis sufferers and their 'carers') experiences unique. What's much more interesting to me now is what makes those experiences the same!

5 CHILD CAREGIVER ACCOUNTS

Sherry

I was 11 when my mum told me that she was going into hospital because her 'headaches' were troubling her. We were on a walk together and I remember her starting to talk as she took my hand to cross the road. I asked her how long she'd be away for, and she told me that she didn't know but it may be a few months. I'm 44 now and she still hasn't come home. I promised her on that walk that I would write to her every day. I kept that promise, writing each night before I went to bed. I wrote until I ran out of paper, but I never heard back. I used to hide the letters under my mattress and, every so often, I would give my dad a carrier bag full of 'My Little Pony' envelopes to give to her. I didn't ever ask him what she said or even if he gave them to her but that feeling when I didn't hear back is one that I'll never forget. My mum had a number of hospital admissions prior to this one. Nobody ever told me what was really happening though. I would just see my dad standing in my mum's spot by the school gate and I'd know that she was gone again.

I had the most loving and devoted dad, who I absolutely adored, and an incredible grandma who would leave her home for months on end to look after me. She even took us into her own home for six years when I left primary school. I can honestly say that I feel truly blessed to have had my dad and my grandma in my life. I was extremely well cared for, and I had positive and loving relationships with my family, but I think it's easy to underestimate the impact that a lack of knowledge about an illness can have on a child. I can completely appreciate why adults might feel apprehensive about talking to a young child about complex mental illnesses – in our case, schizoaffective disorder – but an absence of knowledge is a dangerous thing for anyone. I accepted that my mum was ill, but I blamed myself. I grew up thinking that her 'headaches' could, in some way, be my fault. The unpredictability and uncertainty of this illness is frightening when you lack understanding. I genuinely believe that children need to be told the truth. In January 2018, my husband was diagnosed with throat cancer. He was extremely ill. My own childhood experiences of coping with the illness of a parent shaped the way that I chose to talk to my own children – who, at the time, were five and eight. I made sure that they knew the facts. I made sure that they fully understood that what was happening to their dad was in no way their fault. I ensured that any conversations or phone calls that they might overhear wouldn't frighten them. I used medical terminology, which probably went right over their heads, but my gut feeling was that they could filter the information they didn't need. Obviously, I was censored in my approach. I didn't throw too much at them, but I made sure that they had sufficient understanding to cope. I'm not sure to this day which approach is 'better' (or at the very least, less damaging), but I personally believe that knowledge and an adequate understanding are crucial. And not just for children.

My mum has been placed in various hospitals and supported living accommodations over many years. As a child, I visited her on the occasions when it was felt that she was well enough to see me. It was my choice to go. Sometimes it went well and sometimes it didn't. I have been spat at, sworn at and called names. I have witnessed screaming, crying and other very frightening behaviours, but I have also experienced love, laughter, and some of the most insightful conversations I have ever had. I will always remember sitting with my mum and dad in a hospital family room and laughing like we have never laughed before. It's moments like this that I've held on to. For me, they are enough to help you through the harder times.

I wish my dad were alive to share his perspective right now as he was an exceptional carer. Without fail, he visited my mum every week – no matter where she was placed or if she'd told him to go away the previous week – and she wasn't always that polite about it either! He drove round the city streets night after night, looking for her when she absconded from hospital and went missing, and he did everything to support her in every possible way he could. I remember us driving home from my horse-riding lesson one evening, when I was about 14, and asking my dad if he loved my mum. He told me that he loved her very much, but it was a different kind of love. He explained that he wasn't in love with her like he was before she became so poorly but he had made a promise to her on the day they got married that he wasn't prepared to break. Whenever I question what love is, I always refer to one of my favourite books, *Captain Corelli's Mandolin* by Louis De Bernières:

> *Love is a temporary madness; it erupts like volcanoes and then subsides. And when it subsides, you have to make a decision. You have to work out whether your root was so entwined together that it is inconceivable that you should ever part. Because this is what love is.*

I believe it's these deep entwined roots that keep carers strong.

I don't think I quite fall into a category of a 'carer' because my mum is currently refusing contact with me so I'm unable to do much in the way of active caring. What I can do though, is let her know that I love her. I hope that by simply sending a bar of chocolate or a bottle of fizzy drink, she will know that I care. Last week I sent her a card. I didn't write any words because words just aren't working for us right now. I drew an octopus. Octopuses are solitary, versatile and intelligent creatures. They display an array of fascinating behaviours that intrigue people. They are also alert and dexterous as well as being master escape artists. My mum is an octopus. I hope she realises this. There's a chance she will as she is the queen of metaphors. I recently asked one of her psychologists if the seemingly 'gibberish' phrases she utters are in any way symbolic. She told me that they could be. I now know that they are.

I have been exceptionally lucky for the last 14 years that my mum has received the most amazing care from three incredible hospitals. A few months ago, she was transferred to a new hospital.

She hasn't settled yet and, sadly, I don't even know what she thinks or feels right now, but what I have learnt in these past few months is that carers are valued. Don't get me wrong, I have always been treated with the upmost respect and the skills and the knowledge of the staff supporting my mum have always been nothing short of outstanding, but during my very first visit to my mum's new hospital, I experienced something quite unusual. I am being totally selfish here because for the first time in my life (as a relative of a mentally ill patient that is) someone seemed genuinely concerned about my feelings. My mum had asked to see me, so I arrived at the agreed time with an extra-large bar of her favourite chocolate. As is often the case, she refused to leave her room. The nurse I saw didn't give me an apologetic smile or a few sympathetic words of reassurance. She took me to a room and told me that my mum wasn't being fair to me right now. She put kindness before her illness. The way she instigated a phone call between my mum and I was impressive. She did not try and tell me about an illness that I have grown up with; she listened, and she cared. About me. Not just about my mum this time.

Another positive I can take from my experience of being the carer of a patient at my mum's current hospital is the emphasis on the exchange of information. Not only do they go to great lengths to gather information from me, about my mum, but they also offer monthly meetings for carers to listen to professionals and each other. A recent presentation that I attended about psychosis, cognitive processing and thinking was revolutionary. That probably sounds a bit over the top, but it really did challenge the way I view my mum's illness. The fact that the hospital has staff members with job titles containing the word 'carer' speaks volumes. Even though I'm unable to communicate with my mum right now, I still feel that I am part of her life, and that's something I'm incredibly thankful for.

Being a loved one of a person with any mental or physical illness is difficult. The fluctuating feelings of worry, upset, frustration and guilt (to name just a few because the list is long) can be difficult to manage. Sometimes, I've found it hard not to be selfish. There have been periods where I've had to prioritise the needs of my family – and even myself – over my mum's, and that feels horrible. I have often laid awake at night worrying that I've let her down or that I'm not doing enough, but I guess that's par for the course when it comes to being a carer.

My own life hasn't exactly been free from mental health difficulties. I'm lucky enough to be able to say that I'm doing okay, but that hasn't always been the case. Being unwell myself has taught me the importance of having my symptoms and feelings acknowledged and validated. Judgemental attitudes are a killer for me! I know from my own experience of mental illness that false assumptions and a lack of compassion can be extremely destructive. When I am ill, I am unable to communicate my internal dialogue effectively, so it is a very isolating experience. I really hope that one day I will get the chance to show my mum what I have learned.

Every illness is unique, every relationship is different, and no two sets of circumstances are identical. As carers, we do our best. We make mistakes and we get things wrong. We love, we cherish, we learn, and we forgive. We hold on to memories in the hope that, someday, we will have the opportunity to make some more.

Emilie

My dad has suffered with mental health problems since I was very young. When I was three years old, he was involuntarily sectioned and admitted to a psychiatric ward following an 'acute psychotic episode'. Despite my age at the time, I remember that day vividly.

I'm now 27. Between then and now, my dad has mostly avoided contact with mental health services, and refused professional support, so my mum assumed the responsibility of supporting my dad. I always perceived this responsibility to be heavier and more burdensome than the responsibility of caring for three young children.

Throughout my childhood, I felt constantly frustrated that my family's reality was entirely confined to the homes that we lived in. It was masked so well that our struggle remained invisible to the outside world. When I was young, I used to imagine our house with a big dark cloud looming over only our roof, uncertain about when 'Storm Dad' would next come thundering down.

Home was, sometimes, really happy, frequently terrifying, always tense, and forever unpredictable. At the centre of everything was my dad.

To try to explain how I have coped, or how I am coping, with the experiences I have had growing up with my dad could take me forever. Truthfully, the situation and our relationship feel so complex to me. Despite my best efforts to gain an education about mental health, I still struggle to make sense of my relationship with my dad. I still grapple to explain how my mum, my brothers and I have gotten by. Not only got by, but have somehow actually grown in such positive ways, as a unit and as individuals, despite a family life that I can only characterise as one challenge after another, after another. While growing up, I also never understood how my mum coped, or why she stayed.

Over the years, my own methods of coping have been a mixed bag of good and bad. On reflection, my ways of 'coping' were so dysfunctional at times, that some would certainly question whether they could even be classed as coping strategies. Certainly, it may not have looked like I was coping at all. During my teens, my dad was pretty out of control. His mental health was worse, and he was using drugs most weekends.

I developed an eating disorder (ED) and was seen weekly by a Child and Adolescent Mental Health Service. We discussed how my ED could be seen as a way of trying to gain control over some aspect of an otherwise chaotic home life; a way to *cope*. My ED followed me to university, but during my three years away from home, I began to recover and replace this with more positive ways of coping.

Essentially, I think my ability to cope in a healthier way has been massively influenced by the insight I have gained into mental health: by the educational and career path I chose. It wasn't until I began to understand mental health, and more specifically the many ways in which a departure from good mental health can manifest, that I was able to begin understanding my dad and his behaviour. This wasn't some pivotal moment or a sudden awakening. I worked hard to understand and learn, by continuing further education and choosing to study Psychology. I hoped, one day, to use my understanding to help my dad and 'make everything better' for my family. Being the eldest child and only daughter, I've always felt a moral responsibility to do better and be better, for my mum and brothers.

As my understanding grew, my perspective of my dad actually began to change for the better. The resentment I felt towards him, because of the toll his behaviour had taken on the rest of my family, began to lessen. I'll admit, there are still days when I struggle to be positive about and towards my dad, because sometimes I feel that he makes life so difficult. Now, I think I also have a better understanding of why my mum has stayed. My mum is as much my dad's wife, as she is his sole source of support. He depends on her, and she has an unspoken role to fulfil, a role she would never abandon because she feels my dad is her responsibility.

When it comes to coping, what works for one person will never work for everyone. I also think coping is an ongoing process. Now, how I continue to cope is by having a proactive goal. In my work, I am trying to use my insight from my experiences and education, to make positive changes for people with experiences similar to mine. Every day, I *try* to focus on turning past difficult experiences into positive future outcomes.

Matthew

I almost remember it as yesterday, even though it was around 17 years ago. It was so traumatic. I knew my mother was so unwell due to the phone calls from my sister. I just was not sure what to expect. Working away from home, I often would visit because I worried about my mother, but due to work demands I just could not visit home as before.

Eventually things fell apart at home, and I was not sure what fully happened; all I remember was my sister trying to help my mother, then my sister moving out. When things finally got really bad, I moved back home to see how I could help things. I remember the smashed windows of the house when I arrived back home. It did not make sense to me. Eventually, my sister and I visited the hospital to find out how bad things were with my mother. I could not believe it: my mother was terrified by her surroundings and seemed quite helpless; this was not what I remembered how my mother used to be.

Over time, due to the conversations with consultants on the ward, it was hard to work out what symptoms my mother was experiencing. The doctors also struggled because there was no history of mental health records; this led to several admissions back and forth to the mental health unit. I must admit that I struggled with the relationship between my mother and myself. The mother–son relationship was reversed, and it seemed that I would have to step in and advocate, refer, do more chores and repair situations when things fell apart. I did not think that I would have to care at such a young age. Matters were made more difficult when having also to provide care to my brothers who both have autism. I tried very hard to limit the disruptions to their lives, because I felt that this is what a family is all about, but because of limited resources in the community, we all suffered.

It was only a matter of time before I decided to link up with other carers; it took a long while, but I realised that other carers ended up supporting what I was going through. Only a very few in the community understood about mental illness, but most people stigmatised the situation. Friends eventually moved on, and the wider family kept their distance. My mother lost most of her contacts and became more isolated; it is a sad but common story.

I can only help her so much but need to help myself. I need to make some difference, no matter how small. I engage with fellow carers, and we try to educate each other about carer identity and what it means to support someone with mental health needs. The experience of caring through mental illness has been difficult and unfortunately, I have had to develop a thick skin, but without a carer network I think I would have come off a lot worse.

There is so much work to do and I still worry about the future, but telling our story is a start . . . it's all about educating each other, it's all about connecting with each other.

6 EXTENDED FAMILY CAREGIVER ACCOUNT

Harinder

It has truly been strange to be asked to write a piece from a carer's perspective as when it comes to family, you never see yourself as a carer, probably due to the stigma that is attached to mental ill health and 'looking after family' in the South Asian culture.

Looking back at how everything unfolded, and how my family and I handled everything, still sends shivers down my spine. My cousin had come from India to study in the UK as his previous choice of place didn't go through. We were told about a week before he arrived that he will be staying with us *'please look out for him'*, with no information about any mental health issues. In our South Asian (Indian) culture, this is normal, where families will accept anyone into their homes and look out for them because that is what families do. Throughout our observations, there were certain behaviours which did not make sense to us. We were in regular contact with my cousin's parents. They shared that my cousin had mild depression and the medication he was taking was for the slight (the mild) depression. After a couple of months of sharing with my family that something was not right, and that we needed to get him some help, my cousin's parents and my own family agreed that things were not as they should be and urgent help was needed. We contacted our local General Practitioner and requested that he see my cousin urgently, as we felt clueless on how else we can help, if we did not know what was actually wrong.

I recall pre-warning my family and my cousin's family that I had an inclination that his behaviour and feelings were slightly more than depression. His low and then suddenly high moods were not normal and needed help from doctors and psychiatrists. Being from the South

Asian community and having the combination of British and Indian cultures at home, meant that it was tough to explain to my cousin's family that having mental health issues were not the end of the world. I know there are many people that go through similar things but do not have the support system that we were lucky enough to have had. I was fortunate that my immediate family and I understood and believed that mental health issues were something that needed to be discussed openly; that there was nothing to hide from and there was no shame or the need to feel belittled because of problems.

The five to six months, which had followed my cousin being referred to a psychosis team, was truly the hardest. We, as a family, tried to implement all the suggestions and tasks that were given to us. We tried to involve the whole family approach and have open conversations. We also tried to keep my cousin's family informed to ease the stress on them. I looked up more and more about bipolar, schizophrenia and anything I could find to do with mental health. I took responsibility for ensuring that my cousin was taking his medication on time and regularly.

It was at the point where my cousin started to refuse his medication and his moods became lower (with COVID-19 and lockdown being important factors) that things started to get out of control. Extended family, the mental health team and friends were saying '*you all look exhausted*', '*you are burning out*'. My cousin was placed in respite care, and it was the first time in a year where the house was quiet. It felt like there had been something lifted from our shoulders. As guilty as we felt at that time, it was also the first time we felt we could breathe. It was from here we all had realised that for us to take care of someone, we all had to be healthy, to have enough sleep, and to be energised. Most importantly, our mental health needed to be well looked after before we tried helping someone with theirs.

It has been a rocky two years since the start of this process. Initially, my family and I tried every possible intervention I had learnt in university from my own studies. These ranged from CBT, Acceptance and Commitment Therapy, to yoga, talking walks, going to the gym, and even using mindfulness and talking about expressing feelings on a regular basis. In the end, what helped us and helped my cousin was an open conversation about how trying to look after him, full-time, was difficult. We were not saying that we were unable to; just, sometimes, it was hard for us to manage. We shared that to continue to give support, sometimes each of us needed time away to ourselves, where we could relax and re-energise.

Through this we learnt that as much as we wanted to help and make my cousin 100 per cent better, it would have been difficult, or even impossible, if we did not stop and take time out to look after our own wellbeing, even if it was a simple weekend away, doing an activity we enjoyed, or going on a walk or to the gym. It was, and it is, important for every carer to give themselves that time to rest and heal. Without having that time or taking the time to do so, it negatively affects your own wellbeing in the long run and you are unable to give your 100 per cent in helping someone else recover.

I think the point our situation had started to change was after many open conversations with both my family and my cousin's family. I think these conversations about mental health issues, not just in the South Asian culture but in society as a whole, are vastly important. It had taken a lot of convincing and support from the team to reassure my cousin's family that the strategies put in place (e.g., medication, support teams) were all there to help my cousin feel better and to get better. We found that having open conversations, talking to people, and ensuring we continued with our interests and doing things we enjoyed, helped us get stronger and prepared us to deal with any situation.

I think the most difficult part of being a carer for someone was not actually caring for them, it was the guilt you feel when you are taking time out to look after yourself.

7 SUMMARY AND CONCLUSIONS

This set of first-hand accounts offers insights into the diversity that exists in carer experiences and caregiving impacts in psychosis, and in carers' ideas and suggestions about strategies that have supported their coping.

Despite the variability in the type of caregiving relationships described, there were notable commonalities in carer accounts. These particularly related to an almost overwhelming experience for carers of being and/or feeling in the dark about what was happening and/or what events or psychiatric labels meant during the various phases of the illness, including the initial onset. There was a sense of carers being both an actor and observer in a traumatic life event but with minimal immediate guidance on how best to move forward and cope.

> *At this stage, I became increasingly desperate but completely at a loss as to what to do.*
>
> *[Maggie]*

> *I remember the smashed windows of the house when I arrived back home. It did not make sense to me.*
>
> *[Matthew]*

> *When he became unwell, it was difficult to know how to help him at first.*
>
> *[Abi]*

In many accounts, coping was presented as an ongoing process, but it was not always immediately clear to carers themselves, which was the right or most effective approach to take. It included an acceptance of an illness but recognition that they were not to blame for its existence, and an acknowledgement that the lives of their relative and themselves had changed. However, in the context of these changes and acceptance, carers were able to identify positive elements and carve out a new path for themselves that took account of all their experiences.

> *A carer's life is not the one that we would choose, but it can at least sometimes be interesting.*
>
> *[Philippa]*

> *I had no choice but to re-establish my own life again. I would socialise more with family and friends. I obtained a brand new purpose, such as undertaking new courses, training and improving my interpersonal skills.*
>
> *[Annette]*

> *I needed the confidence and support to return to the things I love. I coped by taking small steps, going for half the class then eventually the whole session.*
>
> *[Amanda]*

The need for and benefits of having good social networks, supportive others, and supportive networks that also included people with their own lived experience of caregiving was a common theme across accounts. While social networks did not prevent difficulties or challenging experiences arising, they allowed carers to feel less isolated, and more equipped and confident in their coping abilities and carer role. Opportunities to engage in activities that were unrelated to the caregiving role but were valued and provided a source of personal joy, were noted:

> *Going to church, where there is a wonderful group of supporting people who know me well, helped me. It allowed me to try and offload all my worries.*
>
> *[Vivien]*

> *Friends equally played a part in my recovery. I was encouraged by the psychologist I worked with to identify the friend I could talk to, the one who I could do things with, the one who offered practical advice and the one who would make me laugh.*
>
> *[Sheena]*

The importance of having their carer role and expertise recognised, and having supportive relationships with clinical teams and individual staff members, were highlighted. Carers, like anyone else, were able to recall the kind words, supportive comments and, empathic tones and gestures, they had received from healthcare staff. Expressions of warmth and acts of kindness, irrespective of magnitude, appeared more likely to stand out and be recalled in the presence of ongoing challenges.

> *Having staff willing to talk to me was important and being able to explain the illness in a way that I understood and being happy to give me information and not hiding behind confidentiality . . . It was staff who listened to me as though I mattered, made me feel valued, saw me as part of the team, and answered my letters.*
>
> *[Pat]*

Though carer accounts were unique and captured different types of relationships, illness durations and phases, and service provision, inherent difficulties associated with psychosis related disorders, remained evident throughout. These included symptoms (e.g., hallucinations) and other illness-related experiences that were often confusing, emotionally draining, and, in some cases, risky. In some accounts, carers' exposure to and reports of risky and challenging behaviours from their relatives, which included acts of aggression and self-harm, were shared.

A sense of feeling helpless in one's own ability to effect change and make things better, which existed against a backdrop of difficulties in accessing the right type of help and in a format that suited the needs of their relative and themselves, was a common feature in accounts. The need for support and assistance from external agencies (e.g., police) were highlighted, as was the importance of agencies being able to deliver care and services that were compassionate, individualised, pragmatic and needs-led.

In their narratives, it was also clear that carers recognised the important contribution of services and treatments. However, parallel concerns about treatment delays, treatment effectiveness and unintended and worrying medication side-effects were often noted, irrespective of whether carers were parents, partners, children or siblings. Some accounts captured the carers' ongoing internal dilemma in weighing up the need for, and benefits of, prescribed treatments versus their perceived psychological and physical harms. Further, the feelings of guilt that some carers experienced as part of their role, and efforts to secure help and treatment for their relative from external agencies, were also highlighted.

The importance of carers equipping themselves with their own information (knowledge) about the illness (including treatments and their impacts), services, care systems and mental health language was frequently noted.

> *I use the Internet to keep up to date with the latest findings on psychosis and have taken some courses to help me. I find that one of the most important aspects in my role is to get as much knowledge about psychosis as I can and get support from carer groups.*
>
> *[Brenda]*

> *Read up on your child's diagnosis and treatment – when you understand more about the illness and the treatment, it will help you manage the situation so much better.*
>
> *[Chris and Terry]*

Carer accounts often captured an intentional and active approach to coping and engaging in behaviours that would support their wellbeing and adjustment.

> *Caring does take it out of you, and you must think about yourself. I had been caring for so long that it became obvious that if I did not start to look after myself, then I would no longer be able to look after him.*
>
> *[Chidem]*

> *Learning to live with psychosis – psychosis is a disability like any other disability; you have to learn to accept and live with it. I wish my son was not disabled but he is.*
>
> *[Chris and Terry]*

> *Therefore, capturing meaningful moments from our daily lives is necessary to stay hopeful in the here and now, rather than wait for a future which may never come.*
>
> *[Agnes]*

Although this publication did not capture all the types of carer relationships, the accounts provided a snapshot of caregiving needs as reported by parents, siblings, partners, children and extended kin, and with variations across gender and racial and ethnic background. Though stories shared overlapping areas, the distinctiveness of the different relationship types (e.g., consider parental carers versus sibling carers), and challenges presented by the specifics of their relationship, were evident. For example, the challenges of navigating the different roles and responsibilities of being a carer and weaving that into a romantic partnership were unique to partner carers. Likewise, there were some unique challenges of being a sibling, where norms and expectations about caregiving contrast significantly with those typically assumed present in other carer relationships (e.g., parental, children). The particular set of difficulties of being a child in a family where there is psychosis is also highlighted.

Globally, deinstitutionalisation and an ongoing shift towards more community-based and local mental health care provision will increasingly rely on family carers to play a key and substantial role in supporting people living with psychosis in local communities. Acknowledging the commonality of needs for carers, alongside the unique experiences of defined carer groups such as partners, siblings, parents, children and carers advancing in age, and/or from racial and ethnic, gender and sexual minority backgrounds, is important if we are to commit ourselves to understanding the different journeys of carers, and their perspectives on what is helpful and nurtures hopefulness.

HELPFUL RESOURCES

1. www.samaritans.org/
2. https://selfhelp.samaritans.org/
3. www.futurelearn.com/courses/caring-psychosis-schizophrenia
4. www.rcpsych.ac.uk/mental-health/treatments-and-wellbeing/caring-for-someone-with-a-mental-illness
5. www.nhs.uk/mental-health/conditions/schizophrenia/overview/
6. www.nhs.uk/mental-health/
7. https://giveusashout.org/
8. https://hubofhope.co.uk/
9. www.nhs.uk/every-mind-matters/
10. www.sane.org.uk/how-we-help/emotional-support
11. www.hearing-voices.org/
12. www.mind.org.uk/
13. www.rethink.org/
14. https://eufami.org/
15. www.youngminds.org.uk/
16. "Cannabis – a time bomb few seem to have heard gone off" https://terryhammond.org.uk/
17. https://nami.org/Home
18. www.kcl.ac.uk/ioppn/research

REFERENCES

Adelman, R. D., Tmanova, L. L., Delgado, D., Dion, S., & Lachs, M. S. (2014). Caregiver burden: a clinical review. *JAMA, 311*(10), 1052–1060. https://doi.org/10.1001/jama.2014.304

Alyafei, A. H., Alqunaibet, T., Mansour, H., Ali, A., & Billings, J. (2021). The experiences of family caregivers of people with severe mental illness in the Middle East: A systematic review and meta-synthesis of qualitative data. *PLoS ONE, 16*(7), e0254351. https://doi.org/10.1371/journal.pone.0254351

Bowman, S., Alvarez-Jimenez, M., Wade, D., et al (2017). The positive and negative experiences of caregiving for siblings of young people with first episode psychosis. *Frontiers in Psychology, 8*(730). https://doi.org/10.3389/fpsyg.2017.00730

Campos, L., Mota Cardoso, C., & Marques-Teixeira, J. (2019). The paths to negative and positive experiences of informal caregiving in severe mental illness: a study of explanatory models. *International Journal of Environmental Research and Public Health, 16*(19), 3530. https://doi.org/10.3390/ijerph16193530

Cooklin, A. (2018). 'Living upside down': being a young carer of a parent with mental illness. *Advances in Psychiatric Treatment, 16*(2), 141–146. https://doi.org/10.1192/apt.bp.108.006247

Del Vecchio, V., Luciano, M., Sampogna, G., De Rosa, C., Giacco, D., Tarricone, I., Catapano, F., & Fiorillo, A. (2015). The role of relatives in pathways to care of patients with a first episode of psychosis. *The International Journal of Social Psychiatry, 61*(7), 631–637. https://doi.org/10.1177/0020764014568129

Doyle, R., Turner, N., Fanning, F., Brennan, D., Renwick, L., Lawlor, E., & Clarke, M. (2014). First-episode psychosis and disengagement from treatment: a systematic review. *Psychiatric Services (Washington, D.C.), 65*(5), 603–611. https://doi.org/10.1176/appi.ps.201200570

Garety, P. A., Fowler, D. G., Freeman, D., Bebbington, P., Dunn, G., & Kuipers, E. (2008). Cognitive behavioural therapy and family intervention for relapse prevention and symptom reduction in psychosis: randomised controlled trial. *The British Journal of Psychiatry: The Journal of Mental Science, 192*(6), 412–423. https://doi.org/10.1192/bjp.bp.107.043570

Gupta, S., Isherwood, G., Jones, K., & Van Impe, K. (2015a). Assessing health status in informal schizophrenia caregivers compared with health status in non-caregivers and caregivers of other conditions. *BMC Psychiatry, 15*, 162. https://doi.org/10.1186/s12888-015-0547-1

(2015b). Productivity loss and resource utilization and associated indirect and direct costs in individuals providing care for adults with schizophrenia in the EU5. *ClinicoEconomics and Outcomes Research: CEOR*, 7, 593–602. https://doi.org/10.2147/CEOR.S94334

Hayes, L., Hawthorne, G., Farhall, J., O'Hanlon, B., & Harvey, C. (2015). Quality of life and social isolation among caregivers of adults with schizophrenia: policy and outcomes. *Community Mental Health Journal, 51*(5), 591–597. https://doi.org/10.1007/s10597-015-9848-6

Jagannathan, A., Thirthalli, J., Hamza, A., Hariprasad, V., Nagendra, H. R., & Gangadhar, B. N. (2011). A qualitative study on the needs of caregivers of inpatients with schizophrenia in India. *International Journal of Social Psychiatry, 57*, 180–194.

Jordan, G., MacDonald, K., Pope, M. A., Schorr, E., Malla, A. K., & Iyer, S. N. (2018). Positive changes experienced after a first episode of psychosis: a systematic review. *Psychiatric Services, 69*(1), 84–99. https://doi.org/10.1176/appi.ps.201600586

Jungbauer, J. & Angermeyer, M. C. (2002). Living with a schizophrenic patient: a comparative study of burden as it affects parents and spouses. *Psychiatry: Interpersonal and Biological Processes, 65*, 110–123.

Kingston, C., Onwumere, J., Keen, N., Ruffell, T., & Kuipers, E. (2016). Posttraumatic stress symptoms (PTSS) in caregivers of people with psychosis and associations with caregiving experiences. *Journal of Trauma & Dissociation: The Official Journal of the International Society for the Study of Dissociation (ISSD), 17*(3), 307–321. https://doi.org/10.1080/15299732.2015.1089969

Koyanagi, A., Oh, H., DeVylder, J., Shin, J. I., Kostev, K., Smith, L., Jacob, L., López Sánchez, G. F., Abduljabbar, A. S., & Haro, J. M. (2022). Psychotic experiences among informal caregivers: findings from 48 low- and middle-income countries. *Social psychiatry and psychiatric epidemiology, 57*(9), 1771–1780. https://doi.org/10.1007/s00127-022-02312-z

Kuipers, E., Onwumere, J., & Bebbington, P. (2010). Cognitive model of caregiving in psychosis. *The British Journal of Psychiatry: The Journal of Mental Science, 196*(4), 259–265. https://doi.org/10.1192/bjp.bp.109.070466

Kuipers, E. & Raune, D. (2000). The early development of expressed emotion and burden in the families of first onset psychosis. In M. Birchwood, D. Fowler, & C. Jackson (Eds.), Early intervention in psychosis (pp. 128–140). Chichester: Wiley.

Kuipers, L. (1992). Needs of relatives of long-term psychiatric patients. In G. Thornicroft, C. Brewin, & C. Wing (Eds.), *Measuring mental health needs* (pp. 291–307). Dorchester: Gaskell.

Martin, J., Butler, M., Muldowney, A., & Aleksandrs, G. (2019). Impacts of regulatory processes on the experiences of carers of people in LGBTQ communities living with mental illness or experiencing a mental health crisis. *Social science & medicine, 230*, 30–36. https://doi.org/10.1016/j.socscimed.2019.03.043

McKenna, A., Hazell, C. M., Souray, R., Cai, W., Man, L. C., Brown, L., Floyd, C., Lyons, N., Widuch, K., James, G., Keay, D., Souray, J., Afsharzadegan, R., & Raune, D. (2022). Do carers of adolescents at first episode psychosis have distinctive psychological needs? A pilot exploration. *The International Journal of Social Psychiatry, 68*(3), 600–609. https://doi.org/10.1177/0020764021992828

Mittendorfer-Rutz, E., Rahman, S., Tanskanen, A., Majak, M., Mehtälä, J., Hoti, F., Jedenius, E., Enkusson, D., Leval, A., Sermon, J., Taipale, H., & Tiihonen, J. (2019).

Burden for parents of patients with schizophrenia: a nationwide comparative study of parents of offspring with rheumatoid arthritis, multiple sclerosis, epilepsy, and healthy controls. *Schizophrenia Bulletin, 45*(4), 794–803. https://doi.org/10.1093/schbul/sby130

National Institute for Health and Care Excellence (NICE). (2014). Psychosis and schizophrenia in adults: prevention and management. Clinical guideline 178. Retrieved from www.nice.org.uk/guidance/cg178.

Norman, R. M., Malla, A. K., Manchanda, R., Harricharan, R., Takhar, J., & Northcott, S. (2005). Social support and three-year symptom and admission outcomes for first episode psychosis. *Schizophrenia Research, 80*(2–3), 227–234. https://doi.org/10.1016/j.schres.2005.05.006

Onwumere, J., Parkyn, G., Learmonth, S., & Kuipers, E. (2019). The last taboo: the experience of violence in first-episode psychosis caregiving relationships. *Psychology and Psychotherapy, 92*(1), 1–19. https://doi.org/10.1111/papt.12173

Onwumere, J., Sirykaite, S., Schulz, J., Man, E., James, G., Afsharzadegan, R., Khan, S., Harvey, R., Souray, J., & Raune, D. (2018a). Understanding the experience of 'burnout' in first-episode psychosis carers. *Comprehensive Psychiatry, 83*, 19–24. https://doi.org/10.1016/j.comppsych.2018.02.003

Onwumere J., Zhou Z., & Kuipers, E. (2018b). Informal caregiving in psychosis: reviewing the impact of patient-initiated violence. *Frontiers in Psychology, 9*, 1530. https://doi.org/10.3389/fpsyg.2018.01530

Palumbo, C., Volpe, U., Matanov, A., Priebe, S., & Giacco, D. (2015). Social networks of patients with psychosis: a systematic review. *BMC Research Notes, 8*, 560. https://doi.org/10.1186/s13104-015-1528-7

Patterson, P., Birchwood, M., & Cochrane, R. (2005). Expressed emotion as an adaptation to loss: prospective study in first-episode psychosis. *The British Journal of Psychiatry, 187* (Suppl48), s59–s64. https://doi.org/10.1192/bjp.187.48.s59

Prasad, F., Hahn, M. K., Chintoh, A. F., Remington, G., Foussias, G., Rotenberg, M., & Agarwal, S. M. (2024). Depression in caregivers of patients with schizophrenia: a scoping review. *Social psychiatry and psychiatric epidemiology, 59*(1), 1–23. https://doi.org/10.1007/s00127-023-02504-1

Revier, C. J., Reininghaus, U., Dutta, R., Fearon, P., Murray, R. M., Doody, G. A., Croudace, T., Dazzan, P., Heslin, M., Onyejiaka, A., Kravariti, E., Lappin, J., Lomas, B., Kirkbride, J. B., Donoghue, K., Morgan, C., & Jones, P. B. (2015). Ten-year outcomes of first-episode psychoses in the MRC ÆSOP-10 Study. *The Journal of Nervous and Mental Disease, 203*(5), 379–386. https://doi.org/10.1097/NMD.0000000000000295

The Schizophrenia Commission. (2012). The abandoned illness: a report from the schizophrenia commission. London: Rethink Mental Illness.

Schofield, N., Quinn, J., Haddock, G., & Barrowclough, C. (2001). Schizophrenia and substance misuse problems: a comparison between patients with and without significant carer contact. *Social Psychiatry and Psychiatric Epidemiology, 36*(11), 523–528. https://doi.org/10.1007/s001270170001

Sin, J., Elkes, J., Batchelor, R., Henderson, C., Gillard, S., Woodham, L. A., Chen, T., Aden, A., & Cornelius, V. (2021). Mental health and caregiving experiences of family carers supporting people with psychosis. *Epidemiology and Psychiatric Sciences, 30,* e3. https://doi.org/10.1017/S2045796020001067

Smith, L., Onwumere, J., Craig, T., & Kuipers E. (2018). Caregiver correlates of patient-initiated violence in early psychosis. Psychiatry Research, *270,* 412–417. https://doi.org/10.1016/j.psychres.2018.09.011

Wildman, E. K., MacManus, D., Harvey, J., Kuipers, E., & Onwumere, J. (2023). Prevalence of violence by people living with severe mental illness against their relatives and its associated impacts: a systematic review. *Acta Psychiatrica Scandinavica, 147*(2), 155–174. https://doi.org/10.1111/acps.13516

Winklbaur, B., Ebner, N., Sachs, G., Thau, K., & Fischer, G. (2006). Substance abuse in patients with schizophrenia. *Dialogues in Clinical Neuroscience, 8*(1), 37–43. https://doi.org/10.31887/DCNS.2006.8.1/bwinklbaur

Worrell, S., Waling, A., Anderson, J., Lyons, A., Pepping, C. A., & Bourne, A. (2023). 'It feels meaningful': How informal mental health caregivers in an LGBTQ community interpret their work and their role. *Culture, health & sexuality,* 1–16. Advance online publication. https://doi.org/10.1080/13691058.2023.2256833

INDEX

Printed in the United States
by Baker & Taylor Publisher Services